W9-CSJ-892

blues harp songbook

by Tony "Harp Dog" Glover

Oak Publications
New York • London • Sydney • Cologne

PHOTOGRAPHS

front cover	Amy O'Neal/Living Blues
4	Susan Martin
15	David Gahr
21	Paul Oliver
23	Roger S. Brown
31	David Gahr
35	David Gahr
43	Diana Davies
45	Ray Flerlage
49	Chris Strachwitz
57	Ray Flerlage
58	David Gahr
61	David Gahr
65	Ray Flerlage
80	David Gahr

Book design by Jean Hammons and Christine Czarny

Calligraphy by
Susan Martin

e d

© 1975 Oak Publications
A Division of Embassy Music Corporation, New York
All Rights Reserved

International Standard Book Number: 0-8256-0157-6
Library of Congress Catalog Card Number: 74-77310

Distributed throughout the world by Music Sales Corporation:

33 West 60th Street, New York 10023
78 Newman Street, London W1P 3LA
27 Clarendon Street, Artarmon, Sydney NSW 2064
Kölner Strasse 199, D-5000, Cologne 90

dedicated to :

Duane Allman
and
Berry Oakley

...two brothers in blues
now on the other end
of the circle...

thanks to:

Herb at Music Sales for patience, calmness, and bread in front...

Galen Michaelson, John Gravlin and Tom Baxter for records, advice, and good jams...

Charles F. Catt, who expressed his opinion of this project by throwing up on the manuscript (and to Siva, who didn't)...

my ancient tape recorder for nearly surviving the heavy punishment...

Wayne 'Fast Fingers' Anthony at KQRS for nimble tape splicing, pitch changing, etc...

Patti Smith ✸ for being a damn good poet and friend...

And most of all to Susan — for calligraphy, listening, counting, transcription help, and enduring...

And anybody else that's got it coming who is omitted here — you know who you are...

Table of Intents

Introduction

Reader, meet *Blues Harp Songbook;* *Blues Harp Songbook*, meet reader.

Okay, now thats over . . .

Dig it, if you're looking for a quick-and-easy course to influencing friends and winning strangers, try Dale Carnegie . . .

If you want to clean up your chops thru the process of imitative discipline by copping some riffs off bluesharp masters, you're in one of the right places.

(The other right place is your own head—but that's between you and your grey matter.)

This is a semi-advanced book . . . it won't be much use if you ain't into blowing and sucking. But if you're part way down the road but temporarily bogged down in a miasma of bad karma, think of this as a possible oasis for your temporal sustenance. (Or as a scheme to con you out of hard-earned pennies. Or as a substitute surrogate father. Or as a way to kill a few months. . . take your pick, it's probably all true.)

In short, Mickey Rooney.

In Front (Again)

I miss forewords in books. They used to tell you stuff you wanted to know —like what was in the book, if it was worth turning the page, if it was worth boosting and/or reading . . . but forewords are getting as extinct as good, cheap booze.

So, in the spirit of nostalgia, neuralgia (with tinges of neurosis)—here's a foreword.

The purpose of this book is to give people who already know the basics of blues harp playing something else to do with their mouths. Tho' it does contain a brief *how-to* section on blues playing, this is intended more as brush-up than in-depth instruction. (If you want that, try *Blues Harp*, also—weirdly enough—written by me.

Most everything I know about harp playing is in there, with more theory and technical stuff as well.) In other words, if you've never played harp before, this book will mostly be useless. But if you got the mojo, it may help.

The book contains a bunch of classic harmonica blues, in styles ranging from folk to jug band to amplified Chicago blues, all written down in a cryptic notation (which looks like gibberish at first)—designed for people who don't read music . . . like myself, Sonny Boy Williamson and most other great harp-men (I always wanted to be in a sentence with Sonny Boy).

The idea is that you can learn a bit about the basics of several widely divergent styles of harp playing by duplicating the riffs on records. And it's true, you can—but don't stop there. The book should be an aid, to help you get your chops together, to clean up your technique, and to help you learn some basic blues riffs. But unless you are satisfied with being a weird kind of jukebox, you'll want to go on and develop your own style, incorporating what you've learned. Imitation ain't creation—and besides, a tape recorder can cover that trip better anyway.

Most of the songs are only partially notated (complete notation would cause this book to weigh 18 pounds, as well as being redundant)—usually the intro, chorus and middle instrumental break (in some cases that's *all* the harpwork on the song). Now and then a verse or two are used. On the instrumental and harp solo numbers, often a basic riff is repeated over and over, with minor rhythmic and melodic variations—the notation here catches the riff and a few variations—you should be able to get the rest. In other words, there are no start-to-finish maps here, but the notation gets the main riffs and general flavor of each piece.

A little plastic record is included—it contains the same parts of the songs that are written out here . . . however a few had to be left off—just wasn't enough room for them all. The people at the publishers tell me that this record is good for a couple hundred plays, however if you have a tape recorder, it might not be a bad idea to tape it, since you'll be playing certain phrases over and over. If you have a two speed reel-to-reel machine, tape it at 7-1/2 IPS—then you can play it back at 3-3/4 IPS—which will lower the pitch one octave, and make each note last twice as long—a real help when it gets fast and heavy. If you don't have a tape machine, but have a player with 16-2/3 speed, you can do the same thing—drop the pitch an octave and double the length of each note. However you do it, I suggest listening to each track a few times while looking over the notation *before* you try to play it. Go thru it once playing along and grab what you can, then go back and work on the licks you missed. And don't get depressed.

A few words of caution: the notation is not guaranteed to be 100% accurate. There are too many factors involved (like turntable speeds varying pitches, etc.) to do more than just go on what your ears tell you—mine just told me the damned roof is leaking again. . .

However, it's absolutely the best I can do it, and it's all guaranteed playable. If you've got perfect pitch, you may hear things I've missed—congratulations. If you don't, who needs it?

Okay, anyway, that's where the book is at. If you're still with me, have fun. If you're not . . . who's reading this?

Blues Harp Mouth Data

(A Compendium of Miscellaneous Stuff Relative
to Playing the Mouth Harp in Blues Style)

Picking a harp; my own personal favorite is still the Hohner ten hole *Marine Band*, tho' they ain't as good as they used to be. The *Bluesharp* model seemed promising, but to my taste it hasn't worked out as well in long term use. It's built on the same style as the *Marine Band*, only the reeds are "looser" and easier to bend—the *Marine Band* needs a bit of breaking in. The *Bluesharp* when new is about equivalent to a broken in *Marine Band* (which makes the former handy to use as a replacement if one of your harps flats out in the middle of a gig)—but it gets soggy feeling after a while and doesn't have the same bite and sweet sting that *Marine Band* usually keeps longer. Once again, it's all up to you—there are several other brands that are cheaper and made differently, so use whatever you're comfortable with and what works for you—after all, it's going in your mouth, so you gotta dig lickin' on it. (A neutral note, not a plug—*Marine Band* was used thru-out in putting this book together, unless otherwise specified.

Basic techniques; Jimi Hendrix was asked what psychedelic music was in the early days of his career in England. He said "it's like playing the wrong notes on purpose." In blues the approach to harp is somewhat on that slipstream—you play a harp in a key different than it's pre-tuned to, on purpose. The reason is fairly simple. Dig the drawing below.

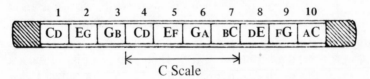

C Scale

This is a diagram of a ten-hole *Marine Band* type harp, tuned in the key of C. *Blow* tones are the larger letters, *draw* or *suck* tones the smaller. Blow in the first hole you get a C tone, draw on the first hole you get a D tone. Notice that the only complete octave on the harp is in holes #4—#7 . . . in the other registers tones are omitted, and/or repeated.

Okay, for the sake of simplification let's say that blues consists of three main chords on the guitar, or whatever you're accompanying. In the key of C they would be: C (the tonic), F (the sub-dominant), and G (the dominant). This is also known in some circles as the I-IV-V progression—C is the first, F the fourth and G the fifth notes in the scale of C. (Most blues are built around this general type of progression, altho' it can get fancy as hell too. For now, leave it here.)

If you were playing along with a guitar player doing a blues in C and using a C harp (this is called *straight* or *first position*), most of your basic notes would be *blow* tones—the only *draw* is the F in hole #5. So what, you mutter. Here's what: in blues there are several flatted notes (called blue notes in one study I read, ain't that hip?)—they would fall in the cracks on the keys of a piano—they aren't built into most Western instruments. You have to make these tones yourself by flatting (or *bending*) the reeds as you play—and it's about 3-1/2 times easier to bend *draw* notes than *blow* notes.

So what we do is find a key that has at least two *draw* tones on our hypothetical C harp. (It is not easy to play a hypothetical harp. Nor sleep in a hypothetical hollow log. Unless you're hypothetical too.) Check the diagram and dig all the G notes—if you play a C harp in the key of G you've got lots of possibilities. (This sounds harder than it is—all it means is you start in a different place than from playing straight harp.) If you play in G on a C harp you also have some chord possibilities that don't exist if you're playing it straight. Besides, it's just a neat thing to do.

In the key of G, a guitar player using the I-IV-V progression would be playing: G (tonic,) C (sub-dominant) and D (dominant). On a C harp that gives you two of the three tones as *draw*, and you can bend them to your livers content.

This is called *cross* or *second position* harp—you're still playing in the same key as the guitar, or whatever . . . only you're using a harp tuned in a key 4 steps above it. And this relationship holds true for all keys. If you go back to the diagram and start with an A tone instead of C (an A harp obviously), the same notes would be skipped and or repeated in the same sequence—only in A. Like this;

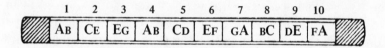

So since harps all have the same *relative* tones, not matter what key they're pre-tuned to, the relationship holds—and you can play a harp tuned a fourth above the guitar key in the guitar key in *cross* style—the basic blues position. Here's a table:

Guitar – Harp Tuning Table

(The last two harp keys are rare, but they do exist and can be ordered. If you need more information on *why*, and things like diatonic and chromatic relationships as well as other tuning tables see *Bluesharp*. But unless you're a fanatic, you probably don't.)

Chops: To be able to play blues on a harp you need a lot of things, strong lungs and tough lips are a couple. But most important are these: learn to get a clear single note, all by itself, without slurping into the ones beside it, and learn to flat or "bend" notes to the exact pitch you need.

The first mentioned above is fairly easy, it just takes playing a lot. You probably got one of those little instruction books with your harp—try playing that junk like *Mary Had A Little Doppleganger, On Top Of Old Porky* etc—it'll help you get into playing clean clear notes. Slurring is a drag. Later you may want to do it on purpose, but at first concentrate on keeping it clean.

Bending notes is more of a problem—some get it right away, some take months. But once you do it you'll never forget how, and you'll be surprised you couldn't do it before. There's a whole physics principle involved in bending notes, but what it comes down to is that you force the air over the reed in a different way, causing the reed to vibrate at a different pitch, which bends the note lower. Try a *draw* note on say hole #2. Now tip the far side of the harp (the side away from your mouth) up—which also causes the side by your mouth to tilt into your lower lip. You should hear a slight bending of tone—thats what you're working for, without tilting the harp. Think of the air that you're sucking in thru the harp as a column, like a straw—usually it just goes back over your tongue into your throat. Try to bend that column of air down to the front part of your lower jaw—maybe drop your tongue to the bottom of your mouth, and draw a bit harder. If you're lucky you'll get a bent note . . . if not keep trying. And don't give up—if I can do it, you can. And I can—but it took awhile to find. Eventually you should be able to get two or three separate tones out of one hole—the regular straight draw tone, and tones slightly lower in pitch. Remember you can only bend notes *down*—to make a missing tone you have to go to the note above it and flat it, or bend it down. As an exercise, after you've been able to bend for awhile, try to play a complete octave, starting on hole #1 blow and going up. When you come to the missing scale note in hole #2 (F on a C harp, for example), bend hole #2 draw down one step (from G to F), then play hole #2 draw straight, without bending . . . and so on, up the scale. See the diagram below:

Once you can do this, you   d you.

Another point to keep in   (two or three holes at once) keep any rhythm sounds   doing a cut-off rhythm with *chunka-chunk* kind of so   —with spaces between the sounds. One of the surest sign   mushy wheeze that comes from sloppy chord wo

There are several effects   tremelo—which is a wavering sound like train's whistles used to make; you can do this by opening and closing your cupped hands around the harp, or by throat and chest *spasm* breathing. Screw around, find out what you can do. The best way to learn to play is to play. If you're driving everybody nuts, go in a closet, go for a walk, hit a subway toilet, whatever, but play every chance you get. The more you do it, the easier it gets. (Once again, for further info on any of the above, see *Bluesharp*, from whence it came.)

Electric Harp: Also known as Chicago style—the harp is played thru its own amplifier—the mike is cupped in the hands with the harp. Mikes and amps are so varied that the best way to find what you want is to just try out a lot of combinations. One thing for *sure*—get a mike that's durable, with a heavy-duty cord. . .or plan on replacing it every other week. As for amps, the main thing is to get a heavy duty speaker, especially if you're gonna be playing loud—those reeds really drive speaker cones. An amp with a reverb on it is nice for that echo-y sound, but not essential. Myself, I like old tube amps better than transistor. I ain't sure if it's just anti-technologyism or what—but the older models sound better to me—they have more bite and character to the sound. Oh well . . .

When playing amplified harp it'll take a while to get your tone settings just right—and that's a totally subjective thing—all I can say is set the treble just under the feedback range, then experiment. You'll be holding a mike with the harp, so you won't be able to do hand tremolos. Work on getting the sound without use of your hands.

And don't get hung up in the power of volume. LOUD may be fun, but it ain't always *good*.

The Cryptic Notation

I'm hip that at first glance this book looks like it's full of gibberish—it is, but it's functional gibberish. This system of writing down harp music was invented for people like myself—and every other harpman I know—who doesn't read standard notation.

It corresponds more-or-less to guitar tablature in that it eliminates one of the steps in converting writing to music sounds. Since harp is such a vocal sounding instrument, each tone (or note) is written out phonetically—the way the note itself sounds as it is played. Under each of these phonetic tones is a number indicating which hole (or holes) is played, and an arrow. An arrow pointing up is a *blow* note (blow in the hole), an arrow pointing down is a *draw* note (suck in that hole). (Wheeew!) Dig:

Da   Daah
2↑   2-3↓

indicates two tones; the first a blow note in hole #2, the second a draw chord, playing holes 2 and 3 simultaneously.

Time (length of notes—how long they're played) is on a relative basis. (Getting into specific tempos like 7/8 time would be confusing to us both). You start with a unit, a basic note. Then notes are timed by their relation to that unit; twice as long, half as long, etc. A unit is shown by a line above the phonetic tones. Two lines means two units, etc. For example:

Dah   Wah   Oooo
2↓   2↑   2-3↓

Here your unit is your first note. You'd play a *draw* tone in #2 and hold it for one unit (or beat, whatever), then a *blow* tone in hole #2 and hold it the same length of time, then a *draw* chord in holes #2 and 3, and hold that twice as long as either preceding note.

This covers whole notes—but there are often half notes or even triplets. Example:

Dah   Dah-Dah   Dah   Da-Da-Da
2↑   1↓   1↓   2↓   1↓ 1↓ 1↓

Again your unit is the first note here. (Remember that the length of the line doesn't matter—it's how many lines there are that count.) You'd play a *blow* tone in hole #2, then 2 *draw* tones in hole #1—each half as long as the first tone. (You could count this: *One-Two-And*). Next a *draw* tone in hole #2, held for one unit—then three *draw* tones in hole #1, each tone being 1/3 as long as the tone in #2 hole; or to put it another way, all three notes together are equal in time to the first note. Right? (Count: *One-Two-And-Ah*.)

There are some variations used in certain pieces. Like:

$$\not\quad \overline{}$$
Dah   Dah-Dah

Here all three notes are equal length, each is a half-unit. Why not write all three under one unit line? That would make the phrase a triplet (3 notes each 1/3 unit) rather than 3-1/2 unit notes. So a crossed unit line means that it's halved. Okay?

You'll see some phrases written like this;

$$\overline{}\quad\overline{}\quad\overline{\overline{}}$$
Dah — Ah-Dah — Dah-Oooo

This shows a whole unit note, followed by two half-unit notes, followed by two more half-unit notes—but the last tone (Oooo) is held for the two units time. The dashes between the tones indicate that it's played all together as one continuous phrase, even tho' separated into different time units. In some pieces this will also be shown by a loop under the tone and hole numbers—it usually means the first tone is held and moves right into the second tone. For example:

$$\overline{\overline{}}\quad\overline{}$$
DA - AHH -Ooo
2-3↓ 2↓ 3↓

shows a chord in holes #2 and 3 being held for two units time, then you play only hole #2 (with a bend in tone) as a continuation of the tone—there is no break. Then move to draw in hole #3.

Bent arrows mean bent notes. How far to bend a tone is something you have to hear—that's what the record is for.

In some pieces you'll see this:

$$\overline{}\quad\overline{\overline{}}\quad\overline{\overline{}}$$ (hold)
Da DAH-Dah-Dah-Dah Ahh-Dahh
2↓ 3↓ 3↓ 2↓ 2↓   1↑ 2↓

The first *DAH* under the second time unit is capitalized to show that it's emphasized—it's played a bit harder or louder than the other notes. Again, listen to the record. The final *Dahh* is followed by (hold)—which means that it's held for a length of time much longer than any other note—rather than pile up time units (in some cases we'd need six or eight) which makes it confusing, you just hold it awhile—the record will help here too.

In some songs there are "ghost" notes—notes that are played very quickly or softly—you may not hear them at first, but they're there. These are usually placed in parentheses ( ).

For convenience and readability, the notation is separated into lines that follow the harp lines as closely as practical—there is often a pause between lines on a page . . . but not always. Sometimes the melody line may run continuously thru several written lines—again, listen to the record as you read along.

An important point: the time here is only for the harp notes—it doesn't count drum beats, guitar licks or rests. You should be able to dig the difference after a couple times thru the notation while the record is playing.

In the songs where there is a band accompaniment, the chord changes used are placed *above* the phonetics—this is just for reference—it helps place where you are in the song structure, it could also be used if you want to try some of the melodies with a guitar player. But they're only there for reference, it's nothing you have to play or worry about. If you don't need them, ignore them.

That about covers the general scheme of things here—specific points for each piece are covered in the introductions.

Some words of consolation: writing phrases down often makes them appear horribly complicated—even tho' they may be very easy to play. Certain pieces here took as long as 8 or 9 hours to transcribe accurately—even tho' I could play them with 10 minutes work. (A little series of triplets that lasts a second and a half might take two hours to dissect and notate.) And, it will probably take awhile to reverse the process—to get that phrase as fast as it should be, with the right attack and emphasis. That's one of the problems in analyzing things—when you break them down to component parts it's easy to lose sight of the whole structure.

Ideally, in time and with practice, you'll be able to hear a phrase a couple of times and then duplicate it yourself—*without* having to consciously break it down and think about which hole, *blow* or *draw*, bend or straight etc. . . . it'll stay music without getting into mechanics. But that only comes with time and experience. By working with the book and record, you should get a good background in learning riffs off records and be able to figure out other pieces not included here. The idea of this book is not to teach everybody who reads it the same twenty songs, but rather to show you how to use your ears, mouth and head to learn from others. The main idea is to aim for connecting your ears to your mouth as directly as possible, keeping the brain out of it as much as possible. (Not to knock brains, they're useful now and then—but they can over-analyze things—sometimes to the point of paralysis.) In other words, try to train yourself to be instinctual. It's not as hard as it might sound—do you have to think about what to do to ride a bike or drive a car?

What matters most is the end result. If you sit down and take a song apart tone-by-tone and are later able to put it back together and play it, good. But if you can eliminate that break-down process almost completely, and play what you hear without having to think on the *how*'s and *why*'s, you're a lot better off.

For what it's worth—I have trouble playing some of the phrases in this book off the page—but from the record there's no problem. I guess all I'm saying is that this is one way to learn music—but there are other ways.

Don't get discouraged, keep after it and you'll get it. But don't get into the rut of always analyzing everything—music is supposed to be fun, too.

The Songs

Okay, now the songs. They're arranged roughly in chronological order—both time and styles. But skip around if you want—whatever works is what's right for you.

Police And High Sheriff

Ollis Martin

Okay, jump right in with a totally obscure solo harp number, by Ollis Martin, recorded in Birmingham Alabma August 6, 1927.

If the tune sounds familiar, it's because it's the same as the chorus to *Do Lord, Do Remember Me* and a cousin to *Gotta Travel On,* both folkie favorites. (The complete version can be found on the *Alabama Country* LP, Origin Jazz Library #14. . .which also contains fine harp songs by George Bullett Williams—his father was a 30-30—and Jaybird Coleman.)

The harp sticks quite close to the vocal melody line, with some variations. The only real hard part is switching from the #4 hole blow to #3 hole bend and back to #4 again—but keep the melody in your ear and it should be third nature.

This is straight harp, played in the key it's tuned to. . .in this case a G harp in G.

Intro:

Doo - Doo   Ah - Ooo   Oooo (Wah) Ahh - Ooo - Ah - A
3↑   3↑   3↓   4↑   4↑   4-5↓   6↑   5↑   4↑   4↑

Wah - Ah - Wah (Hah - A) Hahh
4↑   3↓   4↑   4↑   3↓   3↑

Doo   Doo   Ah - Ah - Ooo - Ooo (Hah) Wahh - Ah - Ooo - Ooo
3↑   3↑   3↓   3↓   4↑   4↑   4-5↓   6↑   5↑   4↑   4↑

Wah - Ah - Ooo - Oooo   Wah - Ooo - Ahhh   Wah - Ahhh
3-4↑   3-4↓   6↑   5↑   3-4↑   3↓   3↑   3-4↑   4↑

Vocal: *Hanging round and fooling bout (-Sure get you down) 3X*
Hanging round and fooling 'bout - Sure get you down
If you hanging round and fooling about too long.

Police and High Sheriff come (Riding down) 3X
Police and High Sheriff come a riding down
And you know you don't want to go.

Doo - Doo   Ah - Ah - Ooo - Ooo (Wah) Ahh - Ooo - Ah - Ah
3↑   3↑   3↓   3↓   4↑   4↑   3-4↓   6↑   5↑   4↑   4↑

Wah - Ah - Wah - (Hah - A) - Hah
4↑   3↓   4↑   4↑   3↓   3↑

Ooo - Wahh   Wah - Ah - Ooo - Wahh (Wah) Ooo - Wah - Ooo - A - wah
3↑   3↑   3↓   3↓   4↑   4↑   3-4↓   6↑   6↑   5↑   4↑   4↑

Wah - Ah - Ooo - Oooo (Wah) - Ooo - Wahh   Wah - Dooo
3-4↑   3-4↓   6↑   5↑   3-4↑   3↓   3↑   3-4↑   4↑

Jug Band Waltz
Memphis Jug Band
-Will Shade-

Next comes another early and important style; jug band harp. Often played in first position (playing harp tuned in same key as guitar, banjo, whatever), jug band harpists usually concentrated on the upper registers—which helped the sound carry over the lower-pitched strings, as well as adding another tone color. There were several jug bands with harp players in the 20's and 30's—and one of the better known was this one, the *Memphis Jug Band*.

Will Shade, the harp player, also wrote most of the songs and was more or less leader of the group. He was born in Memphis, Tennessee on February 5, 1898 and died there in November of 1966. In between he and the band cut a lot of tunes—this one done in September of 1928. The complete version can be found on a good jug band collection: *Origin Jazz Library* Volume #4. (The Kweskin Jug Band recorded a bastardized version on their 2nd LP.)

For many, including me, the hardest problem with this piece is playing in 3/4 time . . . the other problem for cross-harp players is finding their way around in first position. This cut needs a lot of listening to get the timing and inflections right. Think of the notation as a road map—it'll give you an idea, but you need to dig the terrain face-to-face to get where you're going. The line is basically simple . . . the two lines of *Ooo-Woo*'s in the 2nd chorus are actually just one note, played bent and straight, over and over . . . the biggest problem is getting the timing right.

The phrases in parentheses happen fast. The one in the beginning of the 2nd chorus is just a run up the harp—like when you picked it up as a kid and ran it across your mouth.

The band is in C, Shade is blowing a C harp in C. (C-Jam Blues anyone?)

Jug Band Waltz   **Will Shade and Ben Ramey**

1st Chorus: Ahh - A - Wooo   Ahh - hah - Wooo   Ahh - Hah - A - Woo   Ahhh
1↑ 2↑ 3+4↑   5↱ 5↑ 7↑   7↓ 6↓ 6↑ 7↑   6↑

Oooo   Dah - Da - Dee   Ah - Hah - A - Wah   Ahhh
5↑   4↓ 5↑ 6↓   6↑ 5↓ 5↑ 3↓   2↓

Wah - Wah - Ah - Doo   De - De - Da - Dee   Doo
2↓ 3↓ 4↓ 5↓   6↑ 6↓ 7↑ 7↓   6↓

Wah   Wah   Wa - Wah   Wah   Wah   Wahhh
6↑   7↓   6↓ 6↑   5↓   4↓   2+3↑

2nd Chorus: Wah (Ah - Ha - Dah) - Da - Wah - A - Hah   Ooo - Wooo
3↑   5↑ 6↑ 7↑   7↓ 6↓ 6↑ 7↑   8↑ 8↱

Ooo - Woo   Ooo - Woo   Ooo - Woo   Ooo - Woo   Ooo - Woo   Ooo - Woo
8↑ 8↱   8↑ 8↱   8↑ 8↱   8↑ 8↱   8↑ 8↱   8↑ 8↱

Ooo - Woo   Ooo - Woo   Ooo - Woo   Ooo - Woo   Ooo - Woo   Ooo - Wooo
8↑ 8↱   8↑ 8↱   8↑ 8↱   8↑ 8↱   8↑ 8↱   8↑ 7↑

Wah - Ah   Wah - Ah   Wah - Ah   Ahhh   Oooo
7↑ 7↱   7↑ 7↱   7↑ 7↱   7↑   6↓

Ooo   Ah - Ah   Doo   Dah - Dah   Ooo - Wah - Ah - Doo
7↑   8-9↑ 8-9↑   7↓   4-5↓ 4-5↓   7↑ 5↑ 6↑ 6↓

Ah - Wah   Wahh   Wahh   Dahh
5↓ 4↓   3↙   3↓   3+4↑

© Copyright 1929 by Peer International Corporation. Copyright renewed by Peer International Corporation. All rights reserved. Used by permission.

Harmonica Blues
Will Shade

Will Shade was working in a tire plant in Memphis when Sam Charters made a field trip there to record the album this track comes from *American Skiffle Bands*, Folkways FA 2610 in December 1956.*

The *Memphis Jug Band* had long since disbanded, but several of the surviving members got together to cut several tracks for the LP, and reminisce.

This tune gives you an idea of some of the basics of jug band style . . . even tho' there are some mistakes here and there; dropped phrases, shortened bars etc.

For me, this one is much simpler to just play with, rather than think about—reading it back is like reading Serbo-Croatian while going off a ski-jump dead drunk on June 12th on a 350 CC Limey with a broken rear-shock . . . if you know what I mean.

I'm not even sure why this is included here—I guess it's for the rhythm patterns. Oh well. . .

For some obscure reason, the guitar is in B and Shade is playing an E harp in B.

*This track is *not* included on the excerpt record.

From THE STORY OF THE BLUES, by Paul Oliver, Copyright ©Design Yearbook Limited 1969.
Reprinted by permission of the Chilton Book Company, Radnor, PA.

1st: Ah - Da Dee - Dah De - De - Dah De Dah
2↑ 1-2↓ 2-3↑ 2-3↓ 2-3↑ 2-3↑ 2-3↓ 2-3↑ 2-3↓

De - De - Dah De - Dah De - De - Dah De - Dah
2-3↑ 2-3↑ 2-3↓ 2-3↑ 2-3↓ 2-3↑ 2-3↑ 2-3↓ 2-3↑ 2-3↓

Ah - Hah - Ah De - Dah Ah - Hah - Ah De - Dah
2-3↑ 2-3↑ 2-3↓ 2-3↑ 2-3↓ 2-3↑ 2-3↑ 2-3↓ 2-3↑ 2-3↓

De - Dah De - Dah
2-3↑ 2-3↓ 2-3↑ 2-3↓

Ah - Hah - Ah - Dee - Da De - De - De - De - De
3↓ 4↑ 4↓ 6↓ 6↑ 5↑ 5↑ 4↓ 4↓ 4↓

(Da - Da - A)-(Dee - A - Doo)-(A - A - Doo)- Ah Ah - Ah - Hah - Ah
6↓ 6↑ 5↓ 5↓ 5↑ 5↓ 4↓ 4↑ 3↓ 2↓ 1-2↓ 1-2↓ 1-2↓ 1-2↓

(Doo - Ooo - Ah)-(A - Doo) Wah Doo Doo
3↓ 3↓ 2↓ 2↓ 2↓ 2↓ 1↓ 1↓

2nd: Wah - Ah Ah - Ah Hah - Ah - Ah - Ah Wah - Ah - Ah - HAH
1-2↓ 1-2↑ 1-2↑ 1-2↑ 1-2↓ 1-2↑ 1-2↑ 1-2↑ 1-2↓ 1-2↑ 1-2↑ 1-2↓

Ah - Ah - DAH Da - Da - DAH DAH Da - Da - DAH - DAH
1-2↑ 1-2↑ 1-2↓ 1-2↓ 1-2↓ 1-2↑ 1-2↑ 1-2↑ 1-2↑ 1-2↓ 1-2↓

Da Dah DA - DAH - DAH
1-2↑ 1-2↑ 1-2↓ 1-2↓ 1-2↓

Ah - Hah - Dah Dah-HAH- Ah - A Dah - Doo - Ah - Ha
1-2↓ 1-2↑ 1-2↑ 1-2↓ 1-2↑ 1-2↑ 1-2↑ 1-2↓ 1-2↓ 1-2↑ 1-2↑

Da DAH - DAH Dah - Hah - Doo - Ah Dah - Da - Ah Ha - Ah
1↓ 1-2↓ 1-2↓ 1-2↓ 1-2↓ 1-2↑ 1-2↑ 1-2↓ 1-2↓ 1-2↑ 1-2↑ 1-2↑

Glurp Doo Ooo - A - Ooo (hold) Hoo Ooo - Ah - Ooo - Hah
6↓ 6↓ 6↓ 6↓ 6↑ 6↓ 6↓ 6↓ 6↑

Ooo - Ah - Ooo - Hah - A - Wah Wah - Ah
6↓ 6↓ 6↓ 6↑ 5↓ 4↓ 4↓ 4↓

Ah - A - Wah - Ah   Wah - Ah   Wah - Ah   Wah - Ah   Wah - Ah
4↓ 4↵ 4↓   4↵   4↓   4↵   4↓   4↵   4↓   4↵   4↓   4↵

Wah - Ah   Wah   Ah - Hah - Ooo
4↓   4↵   4↓   4↑   3↓   2↓

Ha   Wah - Hah - Ah - Ooo   Hah   Wah   Hah
1-2↑ 4↓   4↑   3↓   2↓   1-2↓ 1-2↑ 1-2↓

Do - Do - Dah - Dah   Do - Do - Dah - Dah
1-2↓ 1-2↓ 1-2↑ 1-2↑ 1-2↓ 1-2↓ 1-2↑ 1-2↑

Ah - Hah - Ah - A   Doo - Doo - Doo - Da - Dah - Dah
5↓   5↑   4↓   6↓   6↓   6↑   5↓   5↑   4↓   4↓

Ah - Hah   Doo - De - De   Doo - De - De - Doo - De - De
4-5↓ 4-5↓ 6↓   6↑   5↓   5↓   5↑   4↓   4↓   4↑   4↓

Dee Ah   Ah   Wah - ah - ah - hah - Ah - Da - Doo - Doo
4↑   3↓   2↓   5↓   5↑   4↓   2-3↑ 2↓   1↓   1↓   1↓

Will Shade and Willie Borum, Memphis, 1961.

K.C. Moan
Memphis Jug Band
-Will Shade-

The final tune with Will Shade is an old jug band favorite, *Kay-Cee Moan.* This is a tune every folkie worth his flat-pick had to know, and it still feels good to play—even if most people nowadays ain't hip what the KC was, much less a moan.

It was originally recorded in 1929 and issued on Victor—the complete version can be found nowadays on the excellent *Anthology of American Folk Music,* Volume No. 3, Folkways FA 2953.

The line is deceptively slow and easy—there are some fast little riffs in there, but it generally follows the vocal melody line. The reason there's no harp on most of the verse is that Shade joined in on harmony.

This is a required course in the Glover School of Semi-Pro Harpology.

The band is in E, he's playing an A harp in E.

Tewee Blackman

Intro Chorus: E Chord
Waaaahh (Hold)   Dah - Doo - Hah - Ah - Doo
3-4↓   3↓   3↙   2↓   2↑   2↓

                 A Chord
Wah - Ah - Hah - A - Doo Dah Doo
3↓   3↙   3↑   2↑   3↑   2↑   3↑

                                   E Chord
Dah Doo Da - Doo - Da - Doo - Dah - Da - Doo
2↑   3↑   2↑   3↑   2↑   3↑   3↑   2↑   3↑

                                      A Chord
Ah   Wah - Ah - Hah - Doo   Wah - Ah - Hah - Ah - Doo
3↓   3↙   2↓   2↑   2↓   3↓   3↙   3↑   2↑   3↑

                                         E Chord
Dah Doo Dah - Doo - Da - Dah - Doo - Da - Da - Da - Doo
2↑   3↑   2↑   3↑   3↑   2↑   3↑   2↑   3↑   2↑   3↑

© Copyright 1929 by Peer International Corporation. Copyright renewed by Peer International Corporation. All rights reserved. Used by permission.

<u>Wah - Ah - Hah - Ah - Doo</u>
3↓   3↓   3↓   2↓   2↓

B⁷ Chord
<u>Wah</u> - <u>Ahh</u> - <u>Oooo</u> (Hold) - <u>Wah - Wah - Ahh -</u>
3↓   4↑   4↓   4↑   3↓   3↙

E Chord
<u>Wah - Ahh - Ooo Dah Da - Da - Da - Dah - Da - Deee</u>
3↓   3↙   2↓   2↓   2↑   1↓   1↓   1↓   2↑   2↓

1st Verse: Vocal:
E Chord
<u>I thought I   heard that   K-C   when   she</u>
<u>Ooo Doo Doo Doo - Ah Doo - Doo Do - Ahh - Doo</u>
4↓   4↑   4↓   4↙   4↓   4↓   4↓   4↓   4↑   4↓

blowed
<u>Wah   Wah - Ah - Wah</u>
3↓   3↓   3↓   2↓

A Chord   E Chord
I thought I heard that K-C when she blowed
A Chord   E Chord
Oh I thought I heard that K-C when she blowed
B⁷ Chord   E Chord
She blows like my woman's on board

E Chord
1st Inst. Break: <u>Waaaaaahhh</u> (Hold thru line)
2+3↓

A Chord
<u>Waaaaahhh</u> (Hold thru line)
3+4↑

E Chord
<u>Waaaaahhh</u> (Hold thru line)
2+3↓

A Chord
<u>Waaaaahhh</u> (Hold thru line)
3+4↑

E Chord
<u>Waaaaahhh</u> (Hold thru line)
2+3↓

B⁷ Chord   E Chord
<u>Do - Wah Ah - Wah - Ah Ah - A - A - Wha</u>
4↓   3↓   2↓   3↓   3↙   3↓   3↙ 3↓   2↓

<u>Doo Da - Da - Da - Da - Dahh</u>
2↓   2↑   1↓   2↑   2↑   2↓

Getting Ready For Trial

Birmingham Jug Band

-Jaybird Coleman-

The last jug band piece is by the *Birmingham Jug Band*. Information was a bit scarce, however the vocalist is very probably Big Joe Williams and the harp player Jay Bird Coleman. Coleman has several harp solo tracks to be found on various anthologies, he was an intense player.

This title was cut in Birmingham around December 1930 and the complete version can be found on *The Great Jug Bands*, Origin Jazz Library No. 4.

There were two harps played here, Coleman's melody, and another which was *mostly* rhythm chords. In a few cases it comes out front and seems a part of the line—in the notation below that's the tones in parentheses. In most cases they could be omitted without losing the melody, but if you can fit them in, fine. Dig the little growl in the harp sound.

The strings are in F here, the harp a B-flat played in F.

<u>Ahh</u> <u>Wahh</u> <u>A - Ahh -</u> <u>Wahh</u>
3↓   2↓   3↓ 3↓   2↓

<u>Ah - A - Woo</u> <u>A - Wah - Ooo</u> <u>Ahh - Woo</u>
4↓ 3↓ 2↓   3↓ 3↓ 2↓   3↓   2↓

<u>Woo - Ah - A - A - Woo</u> <u>Ahh - Wah</u>
2↓ 2↓ 2↑ 1↓ 2↓   2↓   1↓

<u>Wah - Wah</u> <u>Hah - Ah</u> <u>Ooo</u> (<u>Cha -</u>) <u>Ahh - Ooo</u> (<u>Cha</u>)
5-6↑ 5-6↑   4↓   3↓   2↓   1-2↓   1-2↑ 1-2↓   1-2↓

Vocal: *Down in Alabama we was having a trial*
Old Judge Abernath don't spare no lie

<u>Ahh</u> <u>Wah</u> (<u>Cha -</u>)<u>Ahh</u> <u>Wah</u> <u>Ahh - Ooo</u> (<u>Cha -</u>)<u>Ooo</u>
3↓   2↓   1-2↓ 3↓   2↓   2↓ 2↓   2-3↓   6↑

<u>Ooo</u> <u>Wah</u> <u>Ooo</u> <u>Ooo</u> <u>Ooo</u> <u>Cha - Ah - Ooo</u>
4↓   3↓   1↓   6↑   6↑   4-5↓ 3-4↓ 2↓

(<u>Cha -</u>) <u>Ooo</u> - (<u>Cha -</u>) <u>Ah</u>
1-2↓   2↓   1-2↓   1-2↓

Vocal: *Come here big boy, etc.*

1st Inst. Break: <u>Ah - Dah -</u> <u>Ooo - A</u> <u>Wah</u> <u>Ah - Wah -</u> <u>Wah - Doo</u>
3↓ 3↓   4↓ 3↓   2↓   3↓ 3↓   3↓ 2↓

<u>Ah</u> <u>Wah - Doo</u> <u>Wah - Ah - Wah</u> <u>Doo</u>
3↓   3↓ 1-2↓   3↓ 3↓ 2-3↓   1-2↓

<u>Ah - Wah</u> <u>Doo</u> (<u>Cha - Ah - Doo</u>) <u>Ah - Wah</u> <u>Doo</u>
3↓ 3↓   1-2↓   2-3↓ 2-3↑ 2-3↓   3↓ 3↓   1-2↓

<u>Cha - Ah - A - Ah - Doo</u> (<u>Cha -</u>) <u>Ah - Wah</u> <u>Doo</u>
2-3↓ 2-3↓ 2-3↓ 2-3↑ 2-3↓   3-4↓ 4↓ 3↓   1↓

<u>Doo - Doo</u> <u>Wah - Ah - Doo</u> (<u>Chahh -</u>) <u>A - Doo - Ah</u> (<u>Cha</u>)
6↑   6↑   4↓ 3↓ 2↓   1-2↓   2↓ 1↓   2↓   1-2↓

Vocal: *Don't want me mama . . .*

Beautiful City
Sonny Terry

Sonny Terry was born Saunders Teddell, October 24, 1911 near Durham, North Carolina. Nearly blind since childhood Sonny has almost always played music, at first on street corners, later in recording studios with guitarist Blind Boy Fuller. Around the time of Fuller's death in 1940, Sonny met his partner of over 30 years now, Brownie McGhee. Together and separately, they became THE folk-blues musicians—recording and gigging with people like Leadbelly, Woody Guthrie, and Rev. Gary Davis. Sonny has always kept his country roots pretty intact, and he's one of the most explosive "down-home" harpmen in the business.

This cut is a gospel song, with a strong *call-and-response* back and forth swing between harp and voice—in much the same way slide guitarists would let the strings finish a vocal line, Sonny does the same with his reeds. The following is about the first minute of the track, the complete version can be heard on Sonny's solo album Folkways FA 2035. Emphasis has been omitted in the notation—you shouldn't have any trouble hearing it. Work out the rest for yourself. This is a good tune.

Sonny is playing solo harp here, an A harp in the key of E.

Sonny Terry

Intro: Wahh
1+2↓

Doo - Wah	Da - A	Wah - Ah	Wah - Ah	Wah	Ahh -
2↓ 2-3↓	2↓ 2↑	3↓ 2↓	.3↓ 2↓	3↓	2↓

Oooo - Ahh	Dah	Dah - Da - Da	Dah - Da	Da
4↓ 4↓	4↓	4↑ 3↓ 2↓	4↑ 3↓	2↓

```
 ══                    ──   ──   ──   ──   ──        ──
Oooo - Ahh  Dah  Wah - Ah  Wah - Ah  Wah  Ahh - A - Ooo
2↙   2+3↓ 2+3↓ 3↓   2↓  3↓   2↓  3↓   2↓   2↙   1↓
```

```
 ──        ──        ──        ──        ──   ──        ──
Ah - Wah - Dah  Da - Dah - Dee - Ah  Wah  Do - Dah - Dah  Ooo
4↙   4↓   4↑   3↓   4↑   4↙   4↓  3↓   4↑   3↓   2↓   2↓
```

```
 ──   ══
Wahh  Dahh
2+3↓  2+3↓
```

Vocal: *Woooah Lord, what a beautiful city* ‾‾
Wah
2+3↓

Wooh-ho-oh' what a beautiful city God know

```
 ──        ──        ──   ──
Wah - Ah  Wah - Ah  Wah  Doo - Ah
3↓   2↓   3↓   2↓   3↓   2↙   1↓
```

Vocal: *Twelve gates to the city . . . a-hallelujah* ‾‾
Wah
2+3↓

Ah A - men

```
 ──   ──        ──   ──   ──   ──   ──
Dah  Da - Dah - Dee - Ah  Doo  Wah  Doo!
2-3↓ 3↓   4↑   4↙   4↓   4↑   3↓   4↓
```

Vocal: *Hear me talking now*

```
 ──        ──        ──
Oooo  Wah - da - doo  Wah - doo!
4↙   4↓   3↓   4↑   3↓   2↓
```

Vocal: *Yes I mean it now*

```
 ──        ──        ──
Oooo  Wah  A - Doo  wah - doo!
4↙   4↓   3↓   4↑   3↓   3+4↓
```

Vocal: *I done told you now*

```
 ──   ──   ──   ──
Oooo  Wah  A - Doo  Ah - Wahh!
4↙   4↓   3↓   4↑   3↓   2+3↓
```

Vocal: *Which a make twelve gates to the city*
A-hallelujah - Umm, amen

Harmonica Stomp
Sonny Terry

This is another track from the same solo album, Folkways FA 2035—which was recorded in 1952—altho' it could easily have come from 30 years earlier.

This is a fairly simple melody, with various changes—both in line and rhythm patterns. This notation covers the first 3 choruses, you should be able to work out the rest without much problem.

Those triplets in the second chorus happen fast—it's another of those phrases that are easier to play than think about. The "ah" in parentheses at the beginning of many lines are kick-off notes—barely heard, but there.

Sonny is playing an A harp here, in the key of E.

1st: Dah   Waahh
1-2↓ 1-2↓

(Doo) Dah DAH Dah Da OOO - Dah (Ah) DAH Dah - Dah Dah - OOO - Da
2↓   3↓   4↓   4↓ 4↓ 5↑   4↓   2↓   3↓   4↓   4↓   4↓ 5↑   4↓

(Ah) Dah DAH Dah Da DOO - Dah Ah - Wah Dah - DOO - Dah
2↓   3↓   4↓   4↓ 4↓ 5↑   4↓   3↓   3↓   4↓   5↑   4↓

(Ah) Waahh Ah - DOO - Dah (Ah) DAT! - Da - Dah Dah - DOO - Dah,
2↓   3↓   2↓   2↑   1-2↓ 2↑   2-3↓ 2-3↓ 2-3↓ 2↓   2↑   1↓

(Ah) DIT - Di - Dit - Di - DAH Dah - Doo Dah AH - A - Wah Dah - DOO - Dah
1↓   2-3↓ 23↓ 2-3↓ 2-3↓ 2-3↓ 2↓   2↑   1↓   3↓ 3↓ 2-3↓ 2↓   2↑   1-2↓

Ahh - A Wah Dah - Doo Dah Dah - A - Wah Dah - Doo - Dah
3↓   3↓ 3↓   2↓   2↑   1-2↓ 2↓ 2↓ 2-3↓ 2↓   2↑   1-2↓

DAT! Da - Dah – Doo - Dah DAT Dah Dah Dah - Doo - Dah
2-3↓ 2↓   2-3↓   2↑   1-2↓ 2-3↓ 2↓ 2-3↓ 2↓   2↑   1-2↓

2nd: Ah Dah DAH Dah Dah - DOO - Dah *Voc: Woo - Ooo* Dah - OOO - Dah
2↓ 3↓   4↓   4↓ 4↓ 5↑   4↓   4↓   5↑   4↓

Voc: Whoo - Ooo Ah - DOO - Dah *Voc: Woo - Ooo - Ooo* Ah - Doo - Doh
4↓ 5↑   4↓   4↓ 5↑   4↓

Voc: Whoo - Ooo - Ooo Ah *Voc: Whoo - Hoo* Ah - Dah - Doo Dah
4↓   2↓   2↓   2↑   1-2↓

(Ah) DAT - DI - DAH Dah - Doo - Dah (Ah) DIT - Di - DIT - Di - DAH Dah - Doo - Dah
2↑   2-3↓ 2↓ 2-3↓ 2↓   2↑   2-3↓ 2↑   2-3↓ 2-3↓ 2-3↓ 2-3↓ 2↓   2↓   2↑   2-3↓

(Ah) Dit - Di - DIT - Di - DIT - Dit - Di - Dit DAH Dah - Doo Dah
2↑   2-3↓ 2-3↓ 2-3↓ 2-3↓ 2-3↓ 2-3↓ 2-3↓ 2-3↓ 2↓   2↓   2↑   1-2↓

DIT - Di - Di DIT - Di - Di - DAH Dah - Do - Dah
2-3↓ 2-3↓ 2-3↓ 2-3↓ 2-3↓ 2-3↓ 2↓   2↓   2↑   1↓

DIT - Di - Di DIT - Di - Di - DAH Dah - Do - Dah
2-3↓ 2-3↓ 2-3↓ 2-3↓ 2-3↓ 2-3↓ 2↓   2↓   2↑   1↓

$\overline{DIT}$ - $\overline{Di}$ - $\overline{Di}$ - $\overline{DAT!}$ (Rest)　$\overline{Di}$ - $\overline{DAH}$　$\overline{Dah}$ - $\overline{Doo}$ - $\overline{Dah}$
2-3↓　2↓　2↓　2-3↓　　　　2↓　2↓　　2↓　2↑　1↓

$\left(\overline{Ah}\right)$ $\overline{Dah}$　$\overline{Dah}$ - $\overline{Ah}$　$\overline{Dah}$ - $\overline{Doo}$ - $\overline{Dah}$
2↑　3↓　3↓　3↓　2↓　2↑　1-2↓

$\left(\overline{Ah}\right)$ $\overline{DAT}$ - $\overline{Dit}$ - $\overline{Dah}$　$\overline{Dah}$ - $\overline{Doo}$ - $\overline{Dah}$　$\left(\overline{Ah}\right)$ $\overline{DAT}$ - $\overline{Dit}$ - $\overline{Dah}$　$\overline{Dah}$ - $\overline{Doo}$ - $\overline{Dah}$
2↑　2-3↓　2-3↓　2-3↓　2↓　2↑　1-2↓　2↑　2-3↓　2-3↓　2-3↓　2↓　2↑　1-2↓

3rd: $\left(\overline{Ah}\right)$ $\overline{Dah}$　$\overline{DAH}$　$\overline{Dah}$　$\overline{Dah}$ - $\overline{DOO}$ - $\overline{Dah}$　$\left(\overline{Ah}\right)$ $\overline{Dah}$　$\overline{DAH}$　$\overline{Dah}$　$\overline{Dah}$ - $\overline{DOO}$ - $\overline{Dah}$
2↓　3↓　4↓　4↓　4↓　5↑　4↓　2↓　3↓　4↓　4↓　4↓　5↑　4↓

$\left(\overline{Ah}\right)$ $\overline{Dah}$　$\overline{DAH}$　$\overline{Dah}$　$\overline{Dah}$ - $\overline{DOO}$ - $\overline{Dah}$　$\left(\overline{Ah}\right)$ $\overline{Dah}$　$\overline{DAH}$　$\overline{Dah}$　$\overline{Dah}$ - $\overline{DOO}$ - $\overline{Dah}$
2↓　3↓　4↓　4↓　4↓　5↑　4↓　2↓　3↓　4↓　4↓　4↓　5↑　4↓

$\overline{Ah}$　$\overline{WAH}$ - $\overline{Ah}$ - $\overline{A}$　$\overline{Dah}$ - $\overline{DOO}$ - $\overline{Dah}$　$\left(\overline{Ah}\right)$ $\overline{DAAHH}$ - $\overline{Ah}$　$\overline{Doo}$ - $\overline{Dah}$
3↓　3↙　3↓　4↓　4↓　5↑　4↓　3↓　3↓　3↙　2↑　1-2↓

$\left(\overline{Ah}\right)$ $\overline{DAT!}$　$\overline{Dit}$ - $\overline{Dah}$　$\overline{Dah}$ - $\overline{Ooo}$ - $\overline{Dah}$　$\left(\overline{Ah}\right)$ $\overline{DAT!}$　$\overline{Dit}$ - $\overline{Dah}$　$\overline{Dah}$ - $\overline{Doo}$ - $\overline{Dah}$
2↑　2-3↓　2-3↓　2-3↓　2↓　2↑　1-2↓　2↑　2-3↓　2-3↓　2-3↓　2↓　2↑　1-2↓

$\left(\overline{Ah}\right)$ $\overline{DAT!}$　$\overline{Dit}$ - $\overline{Dah}$　$\overline{Dah}$ - $\overline{Doo}$ - $\overline{Dah}$
2↑　2-3↓　2-3↓　2-3↓　2↓　2↑　1-2↓

$\left(\overline{Ah}\right)$ $\overline{DIT}$ - Di - Dit - Di - Di - DIT - Di - Di - DAH　$\overline{Dah}$　$\overline{Doo}$ - $\overline{Dah}$
2↓　2-3↓　2-3↓　2-3↓　2-3↓　2-3↓　2-3↓　2-3↓　2-3↓　2-3↓　2↓　2↑　1-2↓

$\overline{DIT}$ - Di - Dit - Di - DIT - Di - Di - DIT - Di - Di - DAH　$\overline{Dah}$ - $\overline{Doo}$　$\overline{Dah}$
2-3↓　2-3↓　2-3↓　2-3↓　2-3↓　2-3↓　2-3↓　2-3↓　2-3↓　2-3↓　2-3↓　2↓　2↑　1-2↓

$\overline{Dah}$ - Di - $DIT!$　$\overline{Dit}$ - $\overline{DAAHH}$　$\overline{Dah}$ - $\overline{Doo}$　$\overline{Dah}$
2-3↓　2-3↓　2-3↓　2-3↓　2-3↓　2↓　2↑　1-2↓

$\left(\overline{Ah}\right)$ $\overline{Dow}$　$\overline{Dow}$　$\overline{Dow}$　$\overline{Dah}$ - $\overline{Doo}$　$\overline{Dah}$
2↑　3↓　3↓　3↓　2↓　2↑　1-2↓

$\overline{Dah}$ - Di - $DIT!$　$\overline{Dit}$ - $\overline{DAAHH}$　$\overline{Dah}$ - $\overline{Doo}$　$\overline{Dah}$
2-3↓　2-3↓　2-3↓　2-3↓　2-3↓　2↓　2↑　1-2↓

$\left(\overline{Ah}\right)$ $\overline{Dah}$ - $\overline{DAH}$ - $\overline{Dah}$　$\overline{Dah}$ - $\overline{DOO}$ - $\overline{Dah}$　*etc.*
2↑　3↓　4↓　4↓　4↓　5↑　4↓

Dark Road
Sonny Terry & Brownie McGhee

With his partner of three decades, Sonny Terry sort of fills in the gaps between the jug bands and the more urbanized harp styles that followed. Altho Sonny and Brownie are polished performers and entertainers they've managed to avoid getting slick, and their roots are more evident than you might expect. Sonny's style is smoother here, but still has that down-home edge on it.

This track was cut in NYC in 1958—it's on Folkways FW 2327.

The intro phrase is just a little riff where Sonny comes in on the tail end of Brownies guitar intro, to set up his vocal. The harp fills between vocal lines are almost exactly the same all thru the first verse, the changes come on the chord notes. That complicated run in the last line of the E Chord portion of the break is triplets followed by the usual doubles—count it; 1-2-3 1-2-3 1-2-3 1-2 1-2. The last note of that phrase (the one under the A chord) carries over.

The notes in parentheses are "ghost notes"—they're played, but happen so fast that they're barely audible. If you have trouble, omit them at first, but try to work them in later, they're the spice that makes it nice. The notes with exclamation points are cut-off tones—dig the record.

The guitar is in E, Sonny is playing an A harp in E.

Dark Road   **Walter McGhee**

B⁷ Chord
_____
Intro Phrase: *Wah - Ah - Ah - Doo   Wah - Doo*
3↓   4↓   3↓   2↓   1+2↓ 1↓

1st Verse

E Chord
Vocal: *Well my baby left this morning when the clock*
was striking four

_____
Wah - Ah - Ah - Doo   Ah - Wah - Ah - Doo   Dah   Doo - Doo
3↓   4↓   5↑   4↓   3↓   4↓   3↓   2↓   1+2↓ 2↓   2↓

A Chord
Voc: *Well she left this morning when the clock was*
E Chord
striking four

_____
Wah - Ah - Ah - Doo   Ah - Wah - Ah - Doo   Dah   Doo - Doo
3↓   4↓   5↑   4↓   3↓   4↓   3↓   2↓   2+3↓ 2↓   2↓

B⁷ Chord   A Chord
Vocal: *Well, she walked out them old blues*
E Chord
walked in my door

                                              B⁷ Chord
_____
Wah - Ah - Ah - Doo   Ah - Wah - Ah - Doo   Doo   Doo
3↓   4↓   5↑   4↓   3↓   4↓   3↓   2↓   1+2↓ 1↓

Inst. Break: *Spoken:* **Yes she is!**

E Chord
_____
Ah - Ooo   Waaaaah   Wah - Ah
3↓   4↑   4↓   4↓   6↑

_____
Ah - Wah - Ahh   Hah - Ah - Ah - Doo!
4↓   5↑   6↑   5↓   5↑   4↓   3↓

_____
Ooo   Waaaaaah (Hand Tremolo) *Ooo*
3↓   4↓   6↑

                                              A Chord
_____
Wah - Ah - Ah - Ah - Wah - Ah - Doo - Wah - Ah   Doo - Ooo - Ah - Doo
4↓   5↑   6↑   5↓   5↑   4↓   4↓   5↑   4↓   4↓   4↑   3↓   2↓

© Copyright 1965 by Stormking Music, Inc.
All rights reserved. Used by permission.

```
_____    _____    _____
Wah - Ah - Ah      Wah - Ha - Ah      Wah - Hah - Ah - Doo
3↓    4↓    5↑     5↓    5↑    4↓     3↓    3↑    2↑    2↓


_____    _____    _____
Wah - Hah - Ah     Wah - Hah - Ah     Wah -(A -) Hah - Ah - Doo
3↓     4↓    5↑    5↓    5↑    4↓     3↓  (3↙)  3↑   2↑   2↓


A Chord
_____    _____    _____
Wah - Ah!          Wah - Ah!          Wah - Ah!    Ah - Doo   Dah   Doo - Doo
3↓    4↓           3↓    4↓           3↓    4↓     3↓    2↓   2+3↓  2↓    2↓


                   B⁷ Chord
_____    _____    _____    _____
Wah - Ah - Doo - Dah - Doo - Doo - Doo    Doo - Deee
3↑    4↑    4↓    4↓    4↓    4↓    4↓    4↓    6↗

A Chord                                                        E Chord
_____    _____    _____
Wah - Wa   Wah - Wa   Wah - Ahhhh  (Hand tremolo)    Ahh - Ah - Doo
4↙    4↙   4↙    4↓   4↙    4↓                        4↓    3↓    2↓


_____    _____    _____
Wah - Ha - Ah -    Wah - Ah - Ah      Wah -(A -) Ah   Ah - Doo
3↓    4↓    5↑    5↓    5↑    4↓     3↓  (3↙) 2↓   2↑   2↓


                   _____
                   Dah - Doo - Doo
                   2↓    1↓    1↓
```

Sloppy Drunk Blues

Sonny Boy Williamson I

There were two Sonny Boy Williamsons—this one was born John Lee Williamson in Jackson, Tennessee in 1912. He was murdered in Chicago, June 1, 1948, after over a decade of recordings for the Bluebird-RCA Victor labels. His more than 120 sides spanned the *country* style (see especially his album on Blues Classics label with Big Joe Williams) to the *Bluebird Sound*, which some call the forerunner, to Chicago Blues. He influenced most of the next generation of harp men and was generally a very seminal cat. Several albums of his work have been reissued—see the Spleen in the back of the book.

This cut was made in July of 1941, with Blind John Davis on piano and Ransom Knowling on bass—the complete version can be found on *Blues Classics*, LP #3. His style here is fast and raggy. Many of the phrases below are played faster than they can be read.

In line No. 3 of the intro, there are 3 quintuplet phrases—it's just the old *shave-and-a-hair-cut* riff speeded up. This one is hard in spots, but worth working on—it lays a good foundation for later styles.

The band is in C, he's playing an F harp in C.

Sloppy Drunk Blues   **Sonny Boy Williamson**

                                                                    G Chord
Intro: Doo - dah   Ooo   Ooo   Ooo - a - ooo   Ooo - ha   ah
        1↓   2↑   2↙   2↙   2↙   2↑ 1↓   2↑   1↓   1↓

Wah   Da - Dah   Dah - Dah   Dah   Did - le - di - ah - da
2+3↓ 3+4↑ 3↙   4↑   3+4↓   4↓   4↓ 3↓ 2↓ 1↓ 2↑

                        C Chord
Ah - Wha - Oooo
2↓   2↙   2↓

(Did · le - di - ah - da)(Did · le - di - ah - da)(Did - le - di - ah - da)
  3↓   2↓ 1↓ 1+2↑ 1↓   3↓   2↓ 1↓ 1+2↑ 1↓   3↓   2↓ 1↓ 1+2↑ 1↓

          G Chord
Ooo   Ah - Wah
2↓   1↓   1↓

                          C Chord
1st Verse Vocal: **Now I would rather be sloppy drunk**
            F Chord   C Chord
            than anything I know

Dah - Ahh   WAAH   Dah - ah - OOOO   Wah   Doo
3↓   2↓   3↓   2↓   1↓   2↙   1↙   2↙

                    F Chord
Vocal: **You know I'd rather be sloppy drunk**
                    C Chord
         than anything I know

Dah - Ahh   WAAH   Dah - ah - oooo   Wah   Doo - Ah
3↓   2↓   3↓   2↓   1↓   2↙   1↓   2↙   1↙

                G Chord
Vocal: **You know in another half a pint**
                        C Chord
         Woman and you will see me go

© Copyright 1947 by MCA Music, a division of MCA, Inc., 445 Park Avenue, New York, 10022.
All rights reserved. Used by permission.

Wah - Ah   Ahh - Oooo   Wah - a - ha   Doo   Da - Dah
2+3↓ 2+3↑ 4↙   4↓   3↓   4↓ 3↓   2↓   1↓   1↓

C Chord

Inst. Break: WAH - Wah   Wah - Wah   WAH - Ah!
                3+4↓ 3+4↓   3+4↓ 3+4↓   2+3↓ 2+3↓

Wah - Wah   Wah   Oooo   Ooo - Ahh
3+4↓ 3+4↓ 3+4↓ 2↓   2↙   1↓

Dah   Aah   WAH   Dah - ah   OOOO   Wah   Do
3↓   2↓   3↓   2↓   1↓   2↙   1↙   2↙

F Chord

Ahh   Hah - Ah   Wah - Wah   Wah - Wah   Wah - Oooo   Wah
5+6↓   5↓   4↓   3+4↑ 3+4↑   3+4↑ 3+4↑   2+3↑ 1+2↑   2+3↑

C Chord

Wah   Wah   Wah   Oooo - Ooo   Ahh
3+4↓ 3+4↓ 3+4↓ 2↓   2↙   1↓

Dah   Aah   WAH   Dah - ah   OOOO   Wah - Do
3↓   2↓   3↓   2↓   1↓   2↙   1↙   2↙

G Chord

Wah - ah - a   Wah - Wah   Wah - Wah   Ooo - Ooo
2↓   3↓ 3↑   3+4↓ 3+4↓   3+4↓ 3+4↓   2↓   2↓

C Chord

Wah - Wah   Wah - Wah   Ooo - Ooo - Ah
3+4↓ 3+4↓   3+4↓ 3+4↓   2↓   2↙   1↓

G Chord

Wah   Hah - Ah - Hah   WAAAH   Haa   Hah - Ah - Ha   Ah   DAH   Dah
2+3↑ 2+3↓ 2+3↑ 2+3↓   2+3↓   1+2↑ 1+2↓ 1+2↑ 1+2↓ 1+2↓ 1↓   1↓

40

Worried About My Baby
Howlin' Wolf

Howlin' Wolf was born Chester Burnett June 19, 1910 near Tupelo, Mississippi. He got interested in guitar thru hearing the legendary Delta bluesman Charlie Patton, and tho' most known as a guitarist and singer, he was also an accomplished harpman as well.

The second Sonny Boy Williamson (Rice Miller) married Wolf's sister in the 30's, and Wolf's style owes a lot to the earlier recorded style of Rice. The songs included here provide a transition from the country styles to the more urbanized sound that came to characterize Chicago Blues.

Both this cut and the following song, *Dog Me Around* were cut in West Memphis, circa 1948, four years before Wolf's move to Chicago. On both tracks the pianist is Ike Turner, guitar is by Willie Johnson, and Willie Steel is on drums. (The complete version can be found on Crown LP 5240 . . . the same album appears under different names on several budget labels.)

This is another case where notes are played faster than can be read. Notice the accents, and how they're used to make little but significant changes in the two breaks written out here. In some cases instead of single notes, partial chords are used.

The band is in E; Wolf is playing an A harp in E.

Worried About My Baby   **Jules Taub and Chester Burnett**

1st Break Vocal: " – – – at night"

E Chord

WAH - Da - Dah - Dah   DAH - Da - Dah - Dah   DAH - Da - Dah   Dah - Oww
4↓   4↓   4↓   4↓   4↓   4↓   4↓   4↓   4↓   4↓   4↓   4↓   3↓

WAH - Da - Dah - Dah   DAH - Da - Dah - Dah   DEE - Da - Dah   Dah - Oww
4↓   4↓   4↓   4↓   4↓   4↓   4↓   4↓   5↓   4↓   4↓   3↓   2↓

A Chord

WAH - Ah Hah - Ah - DOO - Ah   WAH - Ah - Hah - Ah - DOO - Ah
4↓   4↓   2↓   2↓   3↓   2↓   2+3↓   2↓   2↑   1↓   3↓   2↓

E Chord

WAH - Ah - Hah - Ah - HAH   Wah - Ah - Hah - Ah - DOO
4↓   3↓   2↓   2↑   2↓   3↓   2↓   2↓   2↑   2↓

B⁷ Chord   A Chord

WAH - Ah - Hah - A - Doo - AH   Wah - Ah - Hah - Ah - Doo - Ah
2↙   2↙   2↙   1↙   2↙   1↙   3↓   2↓   2↓   2↑   2↓   2↓

E Chord   B⁷ Chord

WAAAH   DAH - A - Dah   Dah - DAH
2↓   2↓   2↙   2↓   1↓   1↓

Vocal: Give you my money . . .

2nd Break Vocal: (spoken) . . . can't sleep

E Chord

WAH - Da - Dah - Dah   DAH - Da - Dah - Dah   DAH - Da - Dah   Dah - Oww
4↓   4↓   4↓   4↓   4↓   4↓   4↓   4↓   4↓   4↓   4↓   4↓   3↓

WAH - (A) - Ooo   WAH - Da - Dah - Dah   DAH - Da - Dah - Dah   Dah - Da - Doo
4↓   4↙   4↓   4↓   4↓   4↓   4↓   4↓   4↓   4↓   4↓   4↓   4↓

A Chord

AH - Wah - Hah - A - DOO - Ah   Wah - HAH - Ah - DOO - Ah
4↓   3↓   2↓   2↓   3↓   2↓   3↓   2↙   2↑   2↓   2↙

© Copyright 1974 by Modern Music Publishing Co., Inc.
All rights reserved. Used by permission.

E Chord

WAH - Hah - Ah   A - DOO - Ah   Ooo - WAH - Hah - Ah - Doo
4↓   3↓   3↓   2↓   2↓   2↑   3↓   3↓   2↓   2↑   2↓

B⁷ Chord   A Chord

Ooo - Doo - Ah - Doo - WAH   Hah - Doo - A - Wah - Doo
2↓   2↓   1↓   2↓   1↓   3↓   2↓   2↑   2↑   2↓

E Chord   B⁷ Chord

Dooooo   Dah - Da - Dah - Da - Dah - DAH
2↓   2↓   2↓   2↓   2↓   1↓   1↓   1↓

Vocal: *Give you my money . . .*

43

Don't Dog Me Around
Howlin' Wolf

Altho' the song and style here is particularly Wolf-like, the harp breaks use a familiar pattern also frequently used by the second Sonny Boy; the first phrase under the *A* change . . . and also the bends on the *B7* change. On the 2nd break the guitar drowns out the harp in spots, so some approximations are made where the tones weren't totally audible. (The difference between guitar and harp notes is much more hearable if you can play it at half-speed.)

This is a tasty little break and well worth working to get as close to as possible. The song comes from the same sessions and personnel list as the previous one.

The band is in E; Wolf is playing an A harp in E.

Don't Dog Me Around   **Jules Taub and Chester Burnett**

E Chord

1st Break: Waaaaaah (Hold)   Ȧh
3+4↓   2↓

Waaaaah (Hold)   Ȧh - Ȯoo - Ȯoo - (Ah) - Ooo - Wah
3+4↓   4↓   5↓   5↓   4↓   5↓   3↑

A Chord

(A) - WAH - Ah - Ȧ   WAH - Ah - Ȧh - DOO
4↓   4↑   3↓   4↓   4↑   3↓   2↓

                                    E Chord

WAH - Hah - Ȧ   WAH - Hah - Ȧh - Doo   Ah - Wah - Ah - Doo
4↓   4↑   3↓   4↓   4↑   3↓   2↓   2↓   2↑   1↓   2↓

WAH - Hah - Ȧh   WAH - Hah - Ȧh   WAH - Hah - Ȧh - Doo
2↓   2↑   1↓   2↓   2↑   1↓   2↓   2↑   1↓   2↓

Doo - Ah - Doo
2↓   2↑   2↓

            B^7 Chord

Wah - Hah - Ah   Ooo - Ah - Ooo - Ah
2+3↓   1+2↑   1+2↓   3↓   2↓   2↓   1↓

A Chord   E Chord

WAAH - Ah - Ooo - Ȧ   WAH - Ah - Ooo - Ȧ   Wah
3+4↓   3↑   3↓   3↑   3+4↓   3↑   3↓   3↑   2+3↓

Wah - Hah - Ȧ   Wah - Hah - Ȧ   Wah - Hah - A - Doo
2↓   2↓   2↓   2↓   2↓   2↓   2↓   2↓   2↓   2↓

           B^7 Chord

Ah - Dah - Doo
1↓   1↓   1↓

Vocal: *If I treat you . . .*

© Copyright 1974 by Modern Music Publishing Co., Inc.
All rights reserved. Used by permission.

2nd Break: Vocal: *. . . have your way . . .*

E Chord   B⁷ Chord

Wah - Hah - A Wah - Hah - A - Doo A - Ah - Dooo
1+2↓ 1+2↑ 1+2↓ 1+2↓ 1+2↑ 1+2↓ 2↓ 1↓ 1↓ 1↓

E Chord

Waaaaaah (Hold) *Waaah Ah - Oooo*
3+4↓   3↓   4↓ 2↓

Waaaaah (Hold) *- Ah Wah - Ah Dee - Dee - Oooo*
3+4↓   2↓ 4↓ 5↓ 5↓ 5↓   6↑

A Chord

WAH - Hah - Ah WAH - Hah - Ah - Doo
4↓ 4↑ 3↓ 4↓ 4↑ 3↓ 2↓

                                               E Chord

Wah - Hah - Ah Wah - Hah - Ah - Doo Ah - Wah - Ah - Doo
4↓ 4↑ 3↓ 4↓ 4↑ 3↓ 2↓ 2↓ 2↑ 1↓ 2↓

Wah - Hah - A - Wah - Ah Wah - Ah - A - Doo Ah - A - Doo
3↓ 2↓ 1↓ 3↓ 2↓ 3↓ 2↓ 1↓ 2↓ 2↓ 1↑ 2↓

                           B⁷ Chord

Ah - Wah - Hah - Ah - OOO - wah - Hah - OOO - Ah
2+3↓ 3+4↑ 2+3↓ 3+4↑ 4↓ 2+3↓ 2+3↑ 2↓ 1↓

A Chord   E Chord

(A) *Waah - Ah Wah - Hah - Ah - Doo - Ah Wah - Hah - Ah - Doo*
     3+4↓ 3+4↓ 4↓ 3+4↑ 3+4↓ 2+3↑ 2+3↓ 2↓ 2↓ 1↓ 2↓

Wah - Hah - Ah Wah - Hah - Ah Wah - Hah - Ah - Doo
1+2↓ 1+2↑ 2↓ 1+2↓ 1+2↑ 2↓ 2↓ 2↓ 2↓ 2↓

               B⁷ Chord

Doo - Ah - WAH
1↓ 1↓ 1↓

Vocal: *Well I'm going upstairs . . .*

All My Love In Vain

Sonny Boy Williamson II

This is Rice Miller, the second Sonny Boy Williamson—he was born in Glendora, Mississippi around 1897, and died of heart trouble in Helena, Arkansas on May 25, 1965.

He cut many records, including several with English groups backing him—people like the *Animals* and *Yardbirds*. At the time of his death, Rice was on the verge of being "discovered" by the younger white audience.

Rice's first known recordings were made in 1951 for the Trumpet label in Jackson, Tennessee. (Most of these appear on Blues Classics LP No. 9—well worth having—and not included here because of legal hassles.) Sonny Boy was a popular live entertainer in the region, and had a well-known daily radio show at the noon hour.

In 1955 Rice moved north to Chicago and signed with the Checker label, a brother of the Chess label. The song here was one side of his first Checker single—it features Otis Spann, piano, Muddy Waters and Jimmy Rogers, guitars, and Fred Bellow on drums.

Simple in structure and fairly easy to play, the riffs here show a mastery in timing by use of rests and spaces. Sonny Boy let his notes hang out there just the right amount of time—and left enough space between them so they all had room to live. (The complete version is on Chess LP 2CH50027.)

Again, a very personal and definite sound-style—laying down an expressive and evocative feel over some pretty standard changes.

The band is in G; he's playing a C harp in G.

All My Love In Vain   **Sonny Boy Williamson II**

G Chord
Intro Chorus: *Wah - Ah!   Wah - Ah!   Wah - Ah   Wah - Oooo!* (Tremolo)
            3↓ 4↓   3↓ 4↓   3↓ 4↓   3↓ 5↓

C Chord
Dah - Wah - Ah - Dahh   A - A - Wah - Ah   Ah - A - Wah - Ah
2↓   2↓   3↓   3↑   2↓ 2↓   2↓   3↓   2↓ 2↓ 2↓   3↓

G Chord   D Chord
Dah - Ooo   A - Wah - Ah - Doo   Wah - Ah - Ooo (Hold)
2↓   2↓   4↓   4↑   3↓   3↓   3↓   2↓   3↓

C Chord   G Chord
A - Wah - Ah - Da - A   Wa - A - A - Doo
2↓   3↓   3↓   2↓   1↓   3↓   2↓   2↓   2↓

                                    D Chord
Ab   Wah - Wah   Wah - Wah   Wah - Ooo   Wah - Ooo
2↓   2↓   2↓   2↓   2↓   2↓   2↓   1↓   1↓

                    G Chord   C Chord
1st Verse Vocal: *My heart have been broken — And all of*
                    G Chord
my love's in vain

Dah - Oow!   Da - Dah - Ooo   Dah - Oooo   Da - Dah - Ooo
2↓   2↓   2↓   2↓   3↓   2↓   2↓   2↓   2↓   3↓

Vocal: *Heart have been broken — And all my love's in vain*

Dah - Oow   D - Dah - Ooo   Dah - Ooo - Wah
2↓   2↓   2↓   2↓   3↓   2↓   2↓   1+2↓

© Copyright 1955, 1975 by Arc Music Corp.
All rights reserved. Used by permission.

D Chord

Vocal: *But the people's always told me*

C Chord   G Chord

That a woman was a glory for man

                                   D Chord

Ab   Wah - Wah   Wah - Wah   Wah - Ooo   Ah - Wooo
2↓   2↓   2↓   2↓   2↓   2↓   2↓   1↓   1↓

Inst. Break *- after 2nd Verse:*

G Chord

Wa - a - a - ah (Tremolo)   *Ah - A   Wah - Wah - Wah - Wah   Wah - Ooo* (Tremolo and Hold)
     4↓   3↓   2↓   2↓   2↓   2↓   2↓   2↓   2+3↓

Ah - a - a   Oooo (Hold)
  2↓   2↓   1↓   2↓

C Chord

Ab   Wah - Wah   Wah - Wah   Ah - Wah   Wah - Wah
3↓   3↓   3↓   3↓   2↓   3↓   3↓   3↓   2↓   3↓

                     G Chord

Wah - Ah - Ooo - Ah (Hold)   *Ah - a - Ooo   Ahh!*
  2↓   2↓   1↓   1↓   1↓   1↓   1↓   3↓

D Chord   C Chord   G Chord

Wah - Wah - A - Da - A - Ah   A - da - a - ah - ooo - dah - ah - ooo (Hold)
  2↓   2↓   3↓   2↓   1↓   1↑   2↓   2↓   1↓   2↓   1↓   1↓   1↑   2↓

                                       D Chord

Ab   Wah - wah - Wah - Wah   Wah - Ooo
2↓   2↓   2↓   2↓   2↓   1↓   1↓

Vocal: *I'm gonna be tied out . . .*

Moanin' At Midnight

Howlin' Wolf

This track by Wolf is another example of the use of pauses and emphasis by use of accents. It's one of Wolf's trademark guitar-line riffs, his harp is repetitious but exciting.

The song was cut in 1951, probably around Memphis, with Willie Johnson and Pat Hare on guitars, and Willie Steel on drums again. (Complete version on Crown LP 5240.)

Basically this is the same little riff repeated over and over with minor changes, mainly by simple shifting of accents and timing; notice how the time changes after the repeat of the vocal line.

The notes in parentheses are mainly breath notes, they aren't timed but they are played. Here as on most of his sides, dig the unique tone that Wolf gets from the harp—*intense*.

The backing stays in E; Wolf is using an A harp played in E.

Jules Taub and Chester Burnett

Vocal: (falsetto) *Whee - Ooo . . .*

Wah - Ahh - Ah - DOOO *Wah - Ahh - Ah - DOOO*
2↓   2↙   1↓   2↓   2↓   2↙   1↓   2↓

Wah - Ahh - Ah - DOOO *(A) - Wah - Ahh - Ah - DOOO*
2↓   2↙ 2+3↑ 2↓   2+3↑ 2↓   2↙ 2+3↑ 2↓

© Copyright 1951 Modern Music Publishing Co., Inc.
All rights reserved. Used by permission.

(A) - Wah - Ahh - Ah - DOOO   (A) - Wah - Ahh - Ah - DOOO
2+3↑ 2↓ 2↙   2+3↑ 2↓   2+3↑ 2↓ 2↙ 2+3↑ 2↓

(A) - Wah - Ahh - Ah - DOO - (Ah)
2+3↑ 2↓   2↙   1↓ 2↓ 2+3↓

Vocal: Well — somebody knocking on my door

Wah - Ahh - Ah - DOOO   A - Wah - Ahh - Ah - DOOO
2↓ 2↙ 1↓ 2↓   2+3↑ 2↓ 2↙ 1↓ 2↓

A - Wah - Ahh - Ah - DOOO (Ah)
2+3↑ 2↓   2↙ 1↓ 2↓ 1+2↓

Vocal: Well — somebody knocking at my door

Wah - Ahh - Ah - DOOO   (Ah) - Wah - Ahh Ah - DOOO
2↓ 2↙ 1↓ 2↓   2+3↑ 2↓ 2↙ 1↓ 2↓

(Ah) Wah - Ahh - Ah - Doo - Ah
2+3↑ 2↓   2↙ 1↓ 2↓ 1↓

Vocal: Well — I'm so worried I don't know
where to go

Wah - Ahh Ah - Doo Wah (A) Wah - Ahh Ah - DOO
2↓ 2↙ 1↓ 2↓ 1+2↓ 2+3↑ 2↓ 2↙ 2↑ 2↓

(A) Wah - Ahh Ah - Doo WAH - Ahh Ah - Doo
2+3↑ 2↓   2↙ 1↓ 2↓ 2↓ 2↙ 2+3↑ 2↓

(A) WAH - Ahh Ah - Doo
2+3↑ 2↓   2↙ 2+3↑ 2↓

Vocal: Well somebody calling . . .

Checkin' Up On My Baby

Sonny Boy Williamson II

One last number by my personal favorite man, SBW II. No discographical data available, just that it was cut for the Checker label. The backing riff is an often used one, it forms the rhythm line for several blues numbers.

Again fairly straightforward and easy to play, listen to the record. (The complete version can also be found on the double LP set Chess 2CH 50027.)

The band is in A; SBW is playing a D harp in A.

Checkin' Up On My Baby   **Sonny Boy Williamson II**

                                                     A Chord

Intro Chorus: Cha! | Ah - Ooo - Ah - A - OOO! (Band) | Cha | Ooo - Ah - Ooo - WAH
                1-2↓ | 2↓   3↓   4↑   4↑ 4↓ | 1-2↓ | 3↓   4↑   3↓   2↓

                         D Chord   A Chord

Wah | Wah - Ah | Wah - Ah | Ooo | Wah | Wah | Ah - Ooo - Ah - Ooo
3↓   4↑   4↓   4↑   3↓   3↑   2↓   3↓   2↓   3↓   3↓   2↓

                              E Chord   A Chord

Wah | Ah - Wah - Ah - Wah - Ah - Wah | Wah | Ah - A - Ah | Wah
4↓   4↙   4↓   4↙   4↓   4↙   4↓   2↓   3↓   2↓   3↓   2↓

Vocal: I'm checking up . . .

                                        A Chord

Inst. Break: Ahh - Ah | Wah - Ah - Oooo
                 2↓   2↓   3↓   4↙   4↓

Ooo - Wah | Ooo - Wah | Ooo - Wah | Ooo - A - Wah
4↙   4↓   4↙   4↓   4↙   4↓   4↙   3↓   2↓

                               D Chord

Ahhh | Ooo - Wah - Ooo - Ah - Wah
3↓   4↑   4↓   4↑   3↓   3↑

                               A Chord

Wah - Ah | Wah - Ah | Wah - Ah | Ooo - Ah - Ah
4↙   4↓   4↙   4↓   4↙   4↓   4↙   3↓   3↓

                               E Chord

Wah | Wah | Wah | Wah - Ah - A
2↓   2↓   2↓   2↓   2↙   1↓

                               A Chord

Ah - Hah - Ah | Ah - Hah - Ooo
3↓   2↓   3↓   2↓   2↙   2↓

Vocal: I wouldn't call home . . .

© Copyright 1965, 1975 by Arc Music Corp.
All rights reserved. Used by permission.

Hoodoo Man
Junior Wells

Junior Wells was born in Memphis, Tennessee on December 9, 1934. He grew up in an atmosphere of blues and learned from people like Howlin' Wolf, Sonny Boy Williamson (II) and Junior Parker. In the late 40's he moved to Chicago and began his hanging out apprenticeship. When Little Walter left Muddy's band to go on his own, Junior was his replacement for several tours. Then Junior began a long time partnership with guitarist Buddy Guy—they've been backing and recording with each other for years, in various bands.

This track was recorded in 1953 with half of what later became Little Walter's band—Henry Gray, piano, Muddy Waters guitar, David Miles bass, and Fred Below, drums. This was one of six titles issued on the now defunct States label in Chicago; all are top notch early Chicago blues. The version here can be found along with other sides by various artists from the same space-time continuum on Blues Classics LP No. 8.

The phrases in parentheses happen fast—and are almost subliminal—they're there, but they sort of sneak in. The third from last line in the instrumental break is barely audible on the record, the guitar takes the lead there, but with practice you should be able to hear it. Another problem is that because of the harp being amplified it's tones are very close to the slide guitar—you may have to take a couple of dry runs to get the melody line. Altho' separated into different lines here, the break is played almost as one continuous phrase, with only short rests. You have to be pretty familiar with this one to duplicate it.

The band is in A; Junior is playing a D harp in A.

Hoodoo Man   **Junior Wells**

Intro:

Wah	(Hah - A)	Hah	Hah	Hah	(A - Hah) - Do
1-2-3↓	3-4↑	2-3↓	3-4-5↓	3-4-5↓	3-4-5↓ 2-3↓ 3+4↑ 2-3↓

A Chord

Wah	Ah - A	AH - ah - ah -	Ah - ah - ah	Ah - A - Ah
2+3↓	3-4↑ 3+4↓	6↑ 6↑ 6↑	6↑ 6↑ 6↑	6↑ 4↓ 4↑

(Ah - Hah - A - Doo	Wah - Hah - Ah - Doo	(Ah - Wah - A - Hah)
3↓ 4↑ 3↓ 2↑	3↓ 4↑ 4↓ 4↑	2↓ 2↓ 2↓ 3↓

E Chord

Ah	Doo - Doo
1↓	1↓ 1↓

Vocal: Lord I . . .

58

A Chord

Inst. Break: Waaahhh Ah - Ooo
3-4-5↓ 3↓ 2↓

Wahh - A - Dee Ah - A - Dee Ah - Ooo - Ah - Dah - Ah
2-3↓ 4↓ 5↓ 3↓ 4↓ 5↓ 3↓ 4↑ 3↓ 2↓ 1↓

Waaahhh Ooo - Ah
3-4-5↓ 4↓ 3↓

Wah DE - De - De DE - De - De DE - De - De De - Ah - Dah
3+4↑ 6↑ 6↑ 6↑ 6↑ 6↑ 6↑ 6↑ 6↑ 6↑ 4↓ 3↓ 2↓

D Chord

Ah - Ooo - (Wha - Ah) - Ooo Ah - Hah - Wah - (Ah - A)
4↓ 3+4↓ 3↓ 4↑ 3+4↓ 2-3↓ 3-4↑ 2-3↓ 2↓ 1↓

A Chord

Wah - Da - Dee Dah - Da - Dee Dah - De Dah - Ah - A - Doo
3-4↓ 5↓ 5↓ 3-4↓ 5↓ 5↓ 4↓ 4↑ 3↓ 4↑ 3↓ 2↓

Dah De - De De - De Ah - Hah - Ah - Doo Doo - Doo - Da - Doo
3↓ 5↓ 5↓ 5↓ 5↓ 4↓ 4↑ 3↓ 2↓ 2↓ 2↓ 2↓ 2↓

E Chord

Dah Doo - Dah - Ah Ah - Oooo Oooo Oooo Oooo - Ah - A
4↓ 5↑ 4↓ 5↑ 6↓ 6↓ 6↓ 6↓ 6↓ 5↓ 4↓

D Chord   A Chord

Doo Doo - Doo Doo Doo - Doo Do Ah - Wah Ah - Wah - Ah - Doo
6↑ 6↑ 6↑ 6↑ 6↑ 6↑ 5↑ 4↑ 3↑ 3↓ 4↑ 3↓ 2↓

E Chord

Da Wah - Ah Da - Wah - Ah - Ooo Wah - Doo Ah - Doo - Doo
2-3↓ 3-4↑ 3-4↓ 3-4↑ 2↓ 2↓ 3↓ 2↓ 2↓ 1↓ 1↓ 1↓

© Copyright 1965 Wells-Brandom Music
All Rights Reserved. Used by Permission

Standin' Around Crying
Muddy Waters / Little Walter

This is one of the most flat-out *emotional*, low-down, gut-wrenching blues ever recorded. Muddy Waters guitar played slide style, and the harp of Little Walter mix and mesh in a perfect blend of pure driven sound. This track was cut in 1952 when Little Walter was still a regular member of Muddy's band.

Marion Walter Jacobs was born in Alexandria, Louisiana on May 1, 1930. He moved to Chicago while young, and cut his first record for a local label at the age of 17—it was much in the style of the first Sonny Boy Williamson. Walter hung out around South Side clubs and sat in with many of the best Chicago bluesmen, eventually teaming with Muddy Waters. Together they built a style that became known as the Chicago Blues—amplified guitars and harmonicas, but played with down-home soul and funk. On Muddy's earliest recordings with harp, Walter played non-amplified, but later added electricity, which gave him a bigger and fuller sound. Walter was with Muddy for about 5 years, before he left to work with his own band and ideas—and together they made several classic sides—this may be the peak of their ultimate.

(You can find the complete version on an excellent double LP of Muddy Waters older tunes . . . Chess 2CH 60006.)*

This is fairly east to follow along with—dig the use of tremelo tones and how long and hard the lines are—take some deep breaths.

Muddy's guitar is in F; Walter is playing a B-flat harp in F.

*This track *not* included on the excerpt record. You oughta hear the whole thing anyhow.

Intro: Wah   WAH   Ah   Doo (Hold)
        2↓   2↓   1↓   2↵

A - Wah   A - Wah   A - Wah   Ah - Doo   Wah - Ah - Doo
2↵ 2↓   2↵ 2↓   2↵ 2↓   2↵   1↓   3↓   3↵   2↓

WAH   Dah   Wah   Ah - Doo   Ooo - A - DAH (Hold)   Doo
3↓   4↑   3↓   2↓   2↓   2↵   ↵   2↵   1↵

        Da   Dah - Dah - Dah   Ah (Hold)
        2↵   2↵   2↵   2↵   2↵

Vocal: Oh Baby,

Ooo - WAHH (Tremolo & Hold) - Ah - a - Ooo - oo
4↵   4+5↓   4↵   3↵ 4↵   4↓

look how you got me standing 'round crying

Ooo - WAHHH (Tremolo) - ah   Ooo - WAH - ah   Ooo - WAH - ah
4↵   3+4↓   3↓   4↵   4↓   4↵   4↵   4↓   4↵

        Ooo - Wah - ah - Hah - Ooo   Ahh - Ooo
        4↵   4↓   5↓   6↓   6↑   4↑   3↑

Vocal: Oh baby,   O - Ooo   Wah - ah - Ooo
                         4↵ 4↓   4↑   3↑   3↑

look how you got me standing 'round crying

Oooh   Wah - A - Oh - Ooo   Ah - Wha - Doo
4↵   4↵   3↵   4↵   4↓   4↵   3↓   2↓

Wah   Wah - Ah   Ah - Wha   Ah - A - Doo
2↓   2↓   2↵   3↓   2↓   1↓   1↓ 2↵

Vocal: I know I don't love you little girl

        Wah - Wah   Ah - Doo
        2↓   2↓   2↵   3↵

© Copyright 1959, 1975 by Arc Music Corp.
All rights reserved. Used by permission.

Blues Harp Songbook
by Tony "Harp Dog" Glover

Side One
1. Police And High Sheriff
2. Jug Band Waltz
3. K.C. Moan
4. Gettin' Ready For Trial
5. Beautiful City
6. Harmonica Stomp
7. Dark Road
8. Sloppy Drunk Blues
9. Worried About My Baby

Side Two
1. Don't Dog Me Around
2. All My Love In Vain
3. Moanin' At Midnight
4. Checkin' Up On My Baby
5. Hoodoo Man
6. Juke
7. Key To The Highway
8. You Don't Have To Go
9. The Sun Is Shining

For best results, play sound sheet
on top of a standard LP

℗ Oak Publications
A Division of
Embassy Music Corporation, 1975
New York
33 1/3 rpm MONAURAL
726742A&BX

MFD IN U.S.A. BY **EVATONE**® CLEARWATER, FL.
SOUNDSHEETS

But you're always resting on my mind

Wah Ah - A - Wah Ah - A - Wah - Ah - Doo
3↓   3↓ 2↓ 3↓   3↓ 2↓ 4↑   3↓   2↓

A - WAH - A - Doo Wah - Wah Ah - Doo
1↙   2↓   2↙   1↓   2↓   2↓   2↙   2↓

2nd Verse: *Oh baby,* Ooo - WHA - ah - doo - ah
                      4↓   4↙   3↓   4↓   4↓

I ain't gonna be riding around in my automobile

Ooo - WHAHH - oo - ah Ooo - WHAHH Ah - A - Ooh - Wha
4↙   3+4↓   3↓   2↓   4↙   3+4↓   4↓   5↓   6↓   6↑

Ooo - AHH *Oh baby,* Ooo - Ooo Wah - Ah - Dah
4↓   3↑   4↙   4↓   4↑   3↑   3↑

I ain't gonna be riding around in my automobile

Whaa Wha - Da - Dah - da - Dah (Hold) Ahh Ah - Doo
2↓   3↓   2↓   3↓   2↓   3↓   4↑   3↓   2↓

WAH Wah - Wah AH - Wah - Ah - ooo
2↓   2↓   2↓   3↓   2↓   1↓   2↙

You got so many men A - WAH - UHHH! - Dah!
                      6↙ 6↓   6↙   3↑

that I'm afraid you may get me killed

WAH Ah - A - Wah - Ah - Wah Ah - A - Doo A - WAH - Doo
2↓   3↓ 2↓ 3↓   2↓   3↓   4↑   3↓ 2↓   1↓ 2↙   1↙

Wah Wah Ah - Doo
2↙   2↙   2↙   2↓

Juke
Little Walter

This song was Little Walter's first solo effort after working with Muddy—it's success caused him to go out on his own. It was cut in Chicago in 1952 with his band—Louis Miles and David Miles, guitar, and Fred Below, drums. (The complete version can be found on the double Little Walter set, Chess 2CH 60014.)

This is one of the earliest examples of Walter's arranging genius—he builds a simple riff/theme thru several choruses and resolves it with finesse—his tunes were all rehearsed, rather than jammed.

The opening phrases in the first chorus are just runs up the scale. The second chorus features some emphasized tones, contrasted with the lilt on the phrase under the B7 chord. The third chorus is more of the same, with a bit more complicated variations—and the fourth chorus ties it all together, before the break chorus (not included here).

Again, the round sax-like tone is partially the result of the harp being amplified, partially Walter's own chops. You have to play this with spirit to get the right swing to it.

The guitars are in E; Walter is playing an A harp in E.

Juke   **Walter Jacobs**

                                              E Chord
1st Chorus: A̸h ‾Da - Da - Da‾ DEE Dee A̸h ‾Da - Da - Da‾ DEE Dee
              2↓ 3↓ 4↓ 5↓ 6↑   6↑   2↓ 3↓ 4↓ 5↓ 6↑   6↑

              A̸h ‾Da - Da - Da‾ DEE Dee A̸h ‾Da - Da - Da‾ DEE Dee
              2↓ 3↓ 4↓ 5↓ 6↑   6↑   2↓ 3↓ 4↓ 5↓ 6↑   6↑

                                 A Chord
              A̸h ‾Da - Da - Da‾ DEE Dee A̸h ‾Da - Da - Da‾ DEE Dee
              2↓ 3↓ 4↓ 5↓ 6↑   6↑   2↓ 3↓ 4↓ 5↓ 6↑   6↑

                                 E Chord
              A̸h ‾Da - Da - Da‾ DEE Dee A̸h ‾Da - Da - Da‾ DEE Dee
              2↓ 3↓ 4↓ 5↓ 6↑   6↑   2↓ 3↓ 4↓ 5↓ 6↑   6↑

                          B⁷ Chord   A Chord
              A̸h ‾Hah - Ah - Dee - Dee - Doo‾ Ah ‾Hah - Ooo‾ Hah ‾Ah - Doo‾
              3↓ 4↓ 5↑ 5↓ 5↑ 4↓   5↑ 6↑ 5↓   5↑ 6↑ 5↓

                                 E Chord   B⁷ Chord
                          ‾Hah - Ah - Doo‾ ‾Doo - Doo - Ah - Doo‾ ‾Ah - Wah‾
                          3↓ 3↺ 2↓   2↓ 2↓ 2↑ 2↓   1↓ 1↓

                                 E Chord
2nd Chorus: ‾Ah - A‾ ‾DAH - DAH - DAH‾ ‾DAH - Da - DAH - Owww‾
              1↑ 2↑   2↓ 2↓ 2↓   2↓ 2↓ 2↓ 2↺

                          ‾(Ah - A)‾ ‾DAH - DAH - DAH - Ah‾ ‾DAH - Owww‾
                          1↑ 1↓   2↓ 2↓ 2↓ 2↺   2↓ 2↺

                                        A Chord
                          ‾Ah - A‾ ‾DAH - DAH - DAH‾ Da ‾DAH - Owww‾
                          2↓ 2↑   3↓ 2↓ 2↓   2↓ 2↓ 2↺

                                        E Chord
                          ‾Ah - A‾ ‾DAH - DAH - DAH‾ Da ‾DAH - Owww‾
                          2↓ 2↑   2↓ 2↓ 2↓   2↓ 2↓ 2↺

                          B⁷ Chord
                          ‾Ah - Ah - Ah - Doo‾ ‾Ahh - Doo - Doo‾
                          3↓ 4↓ 5↑ 4↓   5↑ 5↓ 5↑

    A Chord   E Chord   B⁷ Chord
    ‾DAH - Dah - Doo - Ah - Doo - Dah‾ ‾Da - Doo - Doo - Ahh‾ Doo Da Da
    3↓ 2↓ 2↺ 1↓ 1↑ 1↓   2↓ 2↓ 2↓ 2↑   2↓ 1↓ 1↓

© Copyright 1952, 1975 by Arc Music Corp.
All rights reserved. Used by permission.

3rd Chorus: Ah - Hah - Ah - Ooooo (Hold)   Ooo - Wah - Ahh - Doo - Ahh - Doo - Ah - A

E Chord

3↓ 4↓ 5↑ 5↓   5↑ 4↓ 4↑ 3↓ 2↓ 2↓ 2↓ 2↓

A Chord

Dow! Dow! Dah - Owww - Ah - A - Oww - A - Ah - Oww!
4↓ 4↓ 4↓ 4↓ 4↙ 4↙ 4↓ 4↙ 4↙ 4↓

E Chord

Dah Doo - Dah - Ahh
2↓ 3↓ 4↓ 2↓

Doo Hah - Ah - Dah - Hah - Ah (- Doo - Hah - A -) Doo Hah Ah - Ah - Doo

B⁷ Chord   A Chord   E Chord

2↓ 2↑ 2↑ 1↓ 2↓ 2↙ 3↙ 4↑ 4↓ 3↓ 2↓ 2↙ 2↑ 1↓

Dah Dah Ahh Doo Dah - Doo

B⁷ Chord

2↓ 2↓ 2↑ 2↓ 1↓ 1↓

4th Chorus: Dooo Dooo Doo - Ah - Hah - Doo - Ah

E Chord

4↓ 4↓ 4↓ 4↙ 4↙ 4↓ 3↓

Ah - Doo - Ooo Dooo Doo - Doo - Dah - Doo - Ahh
4↑ 4↙ 4↓ 4↓ 4↙ 4↙ 4↙ 4↙ 4↓

Doo - Ahhh Doo - Ah - Doo - Ah - Doo - Ahh

A Chord   E Chord

4↙ 4↓ 4↙ 4↓ 4↙ 4↓ 3↓ 2↓

Ah Hah - Ah - Doo - Ah Ah - Hah - Ah - Doo - Ah
5↓ 5↑ 5↓ 4↓ 5↑ 5↓ 5↑ 5↓ 4↓ 5↑

Dah - Dah - (Doo - Ah - Doo) Da - Dah - (Dah - Ah - Doo -) Dah

B⁷ Chord   A Chord   E Chord

1↓ 2↓ 3↓ 4↑ 2↙ 3↓ 2↓ 2↙ 2↑ 1↓ 2↓

Da - Dah - Ah - Dah Ahh - Dah - Dah - Ahh

B⁷ Chord

2↓ 2↓ 2↑ 2↓ 1↓ 1↓ 1↓ 1↓

Key To The Highway
Little Walter

This tune comes from later in Walter's recording career—it was cut in Chicago in 1958 with Muddy Waters and Luther Tucker on guitars, Otis Spann on piano, Willie Dixon, bass, and George Hunter, drums.

The song of course is an old one, first done by Jazz Gillum and Big Bill Broonzy almost two decades earlier—the version here is a nice cross between the country feel of those earlier sides and Walter's usual more high-power style—the harp lines are almost vocal, they mirror the lyrics. The complete version can be found on Little Walters Chess LP 1535. (By the way, the Steve Miller band did a virtual copy of this arrangement on their first album.)

As usual with Walter, the harp is played thru an amplifier, but here tones are rounder and even more sax-like than usual. Real pretty.

The band is in G; Walter is playing a C harp in G.

Key To The Highway   **Willie Broonzy and Charles Segar**

D Chord
Intro: Wah   Ah - A   Doo - Ooo
          4↓   3↓   2↓ 2↙   1↓

C Chord   G Chord
Wah - Ah   Wah - Ah   Wooh   Dah - Ah - Oooh   Oooh
4↙   4↓   4↙   3↓   2↓   2↙   1↓   1↑   1+2↓

                                                      D Chord
DOO   Dah - Da   DOO   Ah - A   Dooo   Doo - Ah   Do
2+3↓ 1+2↑ 1↓   2+3↓ 2↑ 1↓   2+3↓   1↙   1↓   1↓

Vocal: I've got the key . . .

                               G Chord
Inst. Break: Ahh   Wah - Ah   Wah   DOOOOO (Hold)
                2+3↓ 3+4↑ 2+3↓ 1+2↑ 1+2↓

                          D Chord
Ahh   Wah - Ah   OOOOOO
3↓   4↑   3↓   2↙

                    C Chord
Dah   Ooo - Ah - Ooo   Wah - Ah   Waaah   Ah   Dah - Da - Dah
2↓   3↓   4↑   3↓   4↙   4↓   4↙   4↓   3↓   2↓   2↙

             G Chord   D Chord
Wah - Ah - A   Ooo - A - Ahhh (Hold)   Wah - Ah - A   Oooo
3↓   4↑   3↓   4↓   3↓   2↓   2↓   2↙   1↓   1↓

                 G Chord
Dah - DOO   Dahhh (Hold)
1↓   3↓   2↓

Dah - Ah - Ah   Dah   Ooo - Wah - Ah   Wah - Ah - A - Doo
2+3↓ 3+4↑ 2+3↓ 2↙   1↓   1↑   1↓   2↑   2↙ 2↙ 2+3↓

WAAH   Wah - Ah
2↙   2↙   1↓

© Copyright 1941 by Duchess Music Corporation, 445 Park Avenue, New York, 10022.
All rights reserved. Used by permission.

69

You Don't Have To Go
Jimmy Reed

Jimmy Reed was born near Leland, Mississippi on September 6, 1925. He began gigging with his trio in Chicago in 1950, and a few years later they cut the first record for the new Vee-Jay label, an association that would last over twelve years, before the company went out of business. Reed's simple but evocative sound of walking bass lines mixed with high and slow harp got him several hit records; the often recorded *Big Boss Man* and *Ain't That Loving You Baby* were two of the biggest. Reed is still working and recording for Bluesway and smaller specialty labels—but it seems his best work was on the Vee-Jay sides. You can still find many of his numerous albums in bargain bins, some of them have been reissued on other labels.

This cut comes from early in his career—December 1950 in Chicago, to get specific. Reed plays both guitar and harp, Eddie Taylor is on guitar and Morris Wilkerson on drums. The harp here is in a lower register than Reed usually plays, and is very vocal—the intro chorus line anticipates the vocal phrasing very closely. Simple, compact—but very effective use of harp. The complete version was on Vee-Jay LP 1004, it's now included on a Reed reissue album on Buddah—BDS 4003.

The tremolo phrase in the break, under the B-flat change is done with the throat, Reed's hands are busy with the guitar, his harp is in a rack.

The band is in F, Reed is playing a B-flat harp in F.

70

You Don't Have To Go   **Jimmy Reed**

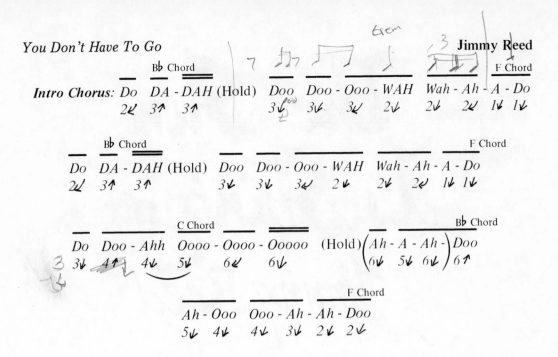

              Bb Chord   F Chord

Intro Chorus: Do DA - DAH (Hold) Doo Doo - Ooo - WAH Wah - Ah - A - Do
           2↙ 3↗ 3↗   3↓ 3↓ 3↙ 2↓ 2↓ 2↓ 1↓ 1↓

              Bb Chord   F Chord

Do DA - DAH (Hold) Doo Doo - Ooo - WAH Wah - Ah - A - Do
2↙ 3↗ 3↗   3↓ 3↓ 3↙ 2↓ 2↓ 2↓ 1↓ 1↓

              C Chord   Bb Chord

Do Doo - Ahh Oooo - Oooo - Ooooo (Hold) (Ah - A - Ah - Doo
3↓ 4↗ 4↓ 5↓ 6↓ 6↓   6↓ 5↓ 6↓) 6↗

                                        F Chord

Ah - Ooo Ooo - Ah - Ah - Doo
5↓ 4↓ 4↓ 3↓ 2↓ 2↓

Vocal: Oh baby . . .

                      F Chord

Inst. Break: Da Doo - Oooo (Hold) Ah - Ooo - Ah
           2↓ 5↓ 5↓   4↓ 3↓ 2↓

Da - A - Dooo (Hold) Ah - Ooo - Ah - Wah
2↓ 3↓ 5↓   4↓ 3↓ 2↓ 2↓

    Bb Chord   F Chord

Ah - WAHAH (Tremolo & Hold) A - Wah - A - Wah - A - Wah Wah - Ah - AH - Do - Ah
4↓ 4+5↓   4↓ 4↓ 4↓ 4↓ 4↓ 4↓ 4↗ 3↓ 2↓ 2↓ 2↓

A - WAH - Hah - A DO
4↓ 3↓ 2↓ 2↓ 1↓

Wah - HAH - Ah - Do A - Wah - Hah - A - Doo
3↓ 4↓ 5↗ 4↓ 3↓ 2↓ 2↙ 2↓ 1↓

DOO Doo Ah Wah - Ah - A - Doo (Hold)
4↓ 3↓ 2↓ 2↓ 2↗ 1↓ 2↓

© Copyright 1954, 1975 by Conrad Music, a division of Arc Music Corp.
All rights reserved. Used by permission.

The Sun Is Shining

Jimmy Reed

This is a more typical Reed style harp number, cut in April of 1957 in Chicago. Eddie Taylor guitar, and Earl Phillips, drums—with Jimmy once again on guitar, and harp in a rack.

The harp here is first position, played mostly up the last octave available. (Complete version can be found on two LP's—either the Buddah BDS 4003, or a recently released collection of Vee-Jay sides on Bluesway BLS-6067.)

The tones here are a bit more intense, at least in terms of attack. The bends on *blow* notes happen more by doing than thinking about, just blow and see what happens. (If you have a cat or dog, beware of side-effects—there must be some weird harmonics in this harmonica key.)

The guitars are in A, Reed is playing an A harp in A.

The Sun Is Shining   **Jimmy Reed, Calvin Carter and Ewart Abner Jr.**

A Chord
Intro Chorus: Dah - Ooo   Dah - Ooo   Dah - Ooo
8↓   8↑   8↑   7↑   8↓   8↑

___   D Chord   ___   A Chord   ═══
Dah - Ah - Ooo   Dah - Ah - Ah - Ooo   Dah - Ah - Eeee
8↑   8↥   7↑   8↑   9↑   8↑   7↑   8↑   9↑   10↑

E Chord   D Chord   A Chord
Ooo - Ah - Ooo   Ooo - Ah - Ooo   Ooo - Ah - Ooo
8↑   8↑   8↓   8↓   8↓   7↑   7↑   8↑   7↑

Vocal: Come on baby . . .

A Chord   ═══   ___
Inst. Break: Dah - Ah - (A) - Oooo (Hold)   Ooo - Wah - Ah
8↑   9↑   9↑   10↑   9↑   8↑   7↑

═══
Dah - Ah - Oooo (Hold)   Ooo - Ooo   Wah - Ah
8↑   9↑   10↑   9↑   9↑   8↑   7↑

D Chord
Ooo - Wah - Ah - Doo   Ooo - Wah - Ah - Doo
8↑   7↑   8↑   7↑   8↑   7↑   8↑   7↑

═══
Dah - Oooo (Hold)   Dah - Ah - Ooo
9↑   10↑   8↥   8↑   7↑

E Chord   D Chord
Dah - Ah - Doo   Dah - Ah - Ooo
8↑   8↑   8↓   8↓   8↓   7↑

A Chord
Ooo - Wah - Ah - Doo
8↑   9↑   8↑   7↑

Vocal: Got a brand new suit . . .

© Copyright 1957, 1975 by Conrad Music, a division of Arc Music Corp.
All rights reserved. Used by permission.

Sitting On Top Of The World

Howlin' Wolf

And a last song by one of the last great bluesmen—Wolf has been in and out of the hospital with heart problems, but at this writing is still gigging, catch him if you can.

This track was cut in Chicago in 1957 with Hubert Sumlin and Jody Williams on guitars, Hosea Lee Kenard on piano, and Earl Phillips on drums.

The tune is another circle closer; an old jug-band number which has remained and evolved thru the years. (There was a C and W version popular not too long ago.) The complete cut can be found on the excellent double LP of older Wolf material Chess 2CH60016.*

This is another vocal-like harp line—the melody is mirrored closely. Try to get that *deep throat* tremolo sound—it's one of Wolf's trademarks.

The band is in F, Wolf is playing a B-flat harp in F.

*Not included on excerpt record.

74

Sitting On Top Of The World   **Chester Burnett**

F Chord
Intro Chorus: Doo   Wah - Ah   Ooo - Wah   Ah   Wah   Ah
2↓   3↓   4↑   4↓   4↓   4↓   4↓   3↓

Bb Chord
Dah   Ooo   Wah - A   Dah   Doo - Wah - Ah   A - Doo
4↓   3↓   4↓   3↓   2↓   4↓   4↓   3↓   2↓   2↓

                    F Chord   C Chord
Doo - Wah   Ah - Doo - Ah   Ah   Wah - Ah   Doo - Ah
2↓   3↓   4↑   4↓   3↓   4↓   3↓   2↓   2↵   1↵

F Chord
Wah - A - Hah   Wah   Ah - A - Wha   Dooo
3↓   4↑   3↓   2↓   2↵   1↓   2↵   2↓

F Chord
Inst. Break: Ah - A - Wahhah (Tremolo & Hold)   Ah   Wah - Ah - Doo
3↓   4↑   3+4↓   4↓   4↓   2↓   3↵

            Bb Chord
Wah - Wah - Doo (Hold)   Ah   Wah - Ah - Doo (Hold)
4↓   4↓   2↓   4↓   4↑   3↓   2↓

                    F Chord   C Chord
Wah   Wah - A   Doo   Wah - Ah   Do   Ah
2↓   2↓   2↓   3↓   3↓   2↓   2↵   1↵

F Chord
Wahh   Wahh   Hah - Ah - A   Wah   Wahh
3↓   3↓   2↓   2↵   1↓   2↵   2↓

© Copyright 1958, 1975 by Arc Music Corp.
All rights reserved. Used by permission.

A Final Word

Pillows

Spleen

Below is a list of all the source albums used for this book.

Alabama Country
OJL-14 ($4.98 . . . Origin Jazz Library/P.O. Box 863/Berkeley, Calif.) Late 20's—early 30's blues . . . harpwork by Ollis Martin, Jaybird Coleman, George Bullet Williams.

The Great Jug Bands
OJL-4 (Same as above.) Good collection of jug band tunes from same era. Includes *Memphis Jug Band, Birminghamn Jug Band*, Noah Lewis, Memphis Minnie, etc.

American Skiffle Bands
Folkways FA 2610. Field recorded in mid-50's, old jug bands revisited. Contains Will Shade and Gus Cannon—but more for nostalgia than music.

Anthology of American Folk Music, Vol. 3
Folkways FA 2953. Contains *Memphis Jug Band*, Sleepy John Estes, Blind Lemon Jefferson, Henry Thomas, John Hurt and more. Fine collection.

Sonny Terry; Harmonica and Vocal Solos
Folkways FA 2035. Has both the harp solos used in this book, seven others. Good folkstyled source.

Brownie McGhee and Sonny Terry Sing
Folkways FW 2327. Has several nice tracks including *John Henry*, done with warmth and style.

Sonny Boy Williamson (I)
Blues Classics—3 (Blues Classics/Box 9195/Berkeley, Calif. 94719 . . . 25 cents for catalogue.) Contains *Sloppy Drunk Blues*, 15 others from late 30's-early 40's. Good re-issue.

Sonny Boy Williamson (II): This Is My Story
Chess 2CH 50027. A double-LP set repackaging of old Checker singles and Chess LP tracks. If you don't have any of SBW II, this is a good place to start.

Chicago Blues; The Early 1950's
Blues Classics-8 (See above.) Junior Wells, Little Walter, John Brim, Baby Face Leroy etc. Fine collection of seminal Chicago blues groups and tunes. Lots of nice harp on here.

McKinley Morganfield a.k.a Muddy Waters
Chess 2CH 60006. Has *Standing Around Crying* plus 23 more, most from the 50's, many with Little Walter or Walter Horton on harp. Another repackage of previously issued LP's—if you have none, start here.

Little Walter; Boss Blues Harmonica
Chess 2CH-60014. Another 2 LP repackage—one LP is the same as *The Best Of* LP issued years back. Contains *Juke*, many other good tracks . . . including 8 instrumentals. Good stuff.

Hate To See You Go; Little Walter
Chess 1535. Has *Key To The Highway*, 14 others from mid-50's. Add to the above LP, you got most of Walter's output.

The Very Best Of Jimmy Reed
Buddah BDS 4003. Has both Reed songs in this book, plus 10 others from original VJ singles. One of the better collections of Reed material.

Chester Burnett a.k.a Howling Wolf
Chess 26H-60016. Still another 2 LP repackage. Has *Sitting On Top Of The World*, 23 others of Wolf's best. Damn good.

The following LP's weren't used in the book, but all have harp on them and might be worth checking out:

Sonny Terry and Brownie McGhee: Back to New Orleans
Fantasy 24708. Two LP's first released on Prestige/Bluesville, now repackaged. Nice.

Joe Williams & Sonny Boy Williamson (I)
Blues Classics-21 (See above.) Has 14 cuts of more down-home styled harp with SBW backing the King of the 9-String, recorded from 1937-47.

The Original Sonny Boy Williamson (II)
Blues Classics-9 (Same as above.) Contains *Come On Back Home*, 15 other early 50's sides from Trumpet label. This is a must.

On The Road Again; Anthology of Chicago Blues 1947-54
Muskadine 100 (Adevent Productions/P.O. Box 635/Manhattan Beach, Calif. 90266) Contains Little Walters earliest recordings, also Baby Face Leroy (with Muddy & Walter), Johnny Shines and John Brim. A specialized anthology for fans of Muddy's early sound.

Jimmy Rogers; Chicago Bound
Chess 407. Rogers was guitar player for Muddy Waters for years—here he's backed by most of Muddy's band, including Little Walter—14 tracks of the best of 2nd line Chicago Blues.

Raining In My Heart; Slim Harpo
Excello 8003. Has title song, 11 more, including *King Bee*. This track also available on *Best Of* LP's.

Junior Wells; It's My Life Baby
Vanguard VSD 79231. A half-studio, half-live LP (Peppers Lounge). The music isn't that dynamite, but the feeling of a south side bar is there. 12 tracks with Buddy Guy on guitar.

And the list could go on and on—there are many reissue labels, with new catalogues every day. Best bet is to check out your nearest specialty record shop, or send off for catalogues.

You might also check out a couple of magazines; *Blues Unlimited*, the house organ of a bunch of semi-berserk English Blues fanatics—it has more information than you'll ever need on a plethora of obscure bluesmen . . . or *Living Blues*, a mag out of Chicago with a more rational approach. (They had an interesting interview with Little Walter a few issues back. Done before he died.)

Record Permissions

Side 1

Police and High Sheriff/ Ollis Martin.
From Origin Jazz Library recording

Jug Band Waltz/ Memphis Jug Band-Will Shade.
From Origin Jazz Library recording.
Used by permission of Peer International Corporation.

K.C. Moan/ Memphis Jug Band—Will Shade.
Used by permission of Folkways Records
and Peer International Corporation.

Gettin' Ready For Trial/ Birmingham Jug Band.
From Origin Jazz Library recording.

Beautiful City/ Sonny Terry.
Used by permission of Folkways Records.

Harmonica Stomp/ Sonny Terry.
Used by permission of Folkways Records.

Dark Road/ Sonny Terry and Brownie McGhee.
Used by permission of Folkways Records
and Stormking Music Inc.

Sloppy Drunk Blues/ Sonny Boy Williamson I.
From Blues Classics LP No. 3*.
Used by permission of MCA Music, A Division of MCA, Inc.

Worried About My Baby/ Chester Burnett (Howlin' Wolf).
From recording on Crown Records.
Used by permission of Modern Publishing Co., Inc.

Side 2

Don't Dog Me Around/ Chester Burnett (Howlin' Wolf).
From recording on Crown Records.
Used by permission of Modern Music Publishing Co., Inc.

All My Love In Vain/ Sonny Boy Williamson II.
Used by permission of Chess/Janus Records
Division of GRT Corporation and Arc Music Corp.

Moanin' At Midnight/ Chester Burnett (Howlin' Wolf).
From recording on Crown Records.
Used by permission of Modern Music Publishing Co., Inc.

Checkin' Up On My Baby/ Sonny Boy Williamson II.
Used by permission of Chess/Janus Records,
Division of GRT Corporation and Arc Music Corp.

Hoodoo Man/ Junior Wells. From Blues Classics LP No. 8*.
Used by Permission of Richard Waterman:
Wells-Brandom Music.

Juke/ Little Walter.
Used by permission of Chess/Janus Records,
Division of GRT Corporation and Arc Music Corp.

Key To The Highway/ Little Walter. Used by permission of Chess/Janus Records,
Division of GRT Corporation and Duchess Music Corporation.

You Don't Have to Go/ Jimmy Reed.
Used by permission of Buddah Records and
Conrad Music, Division of Arc Music Corp.

The Sun Is Shining/ Jimmy Reed.
Used by permission of Buddah Records and
Conrad Music, Division of Arc Music Corp.

*A complete catalog of over 140 blues, folk and jazz LPs, and a copy of the Arhoolie Occasional are yours by
sending twenty-five cents to: Arhoolie, Box 9195, Berkeley, Ca. 94709.